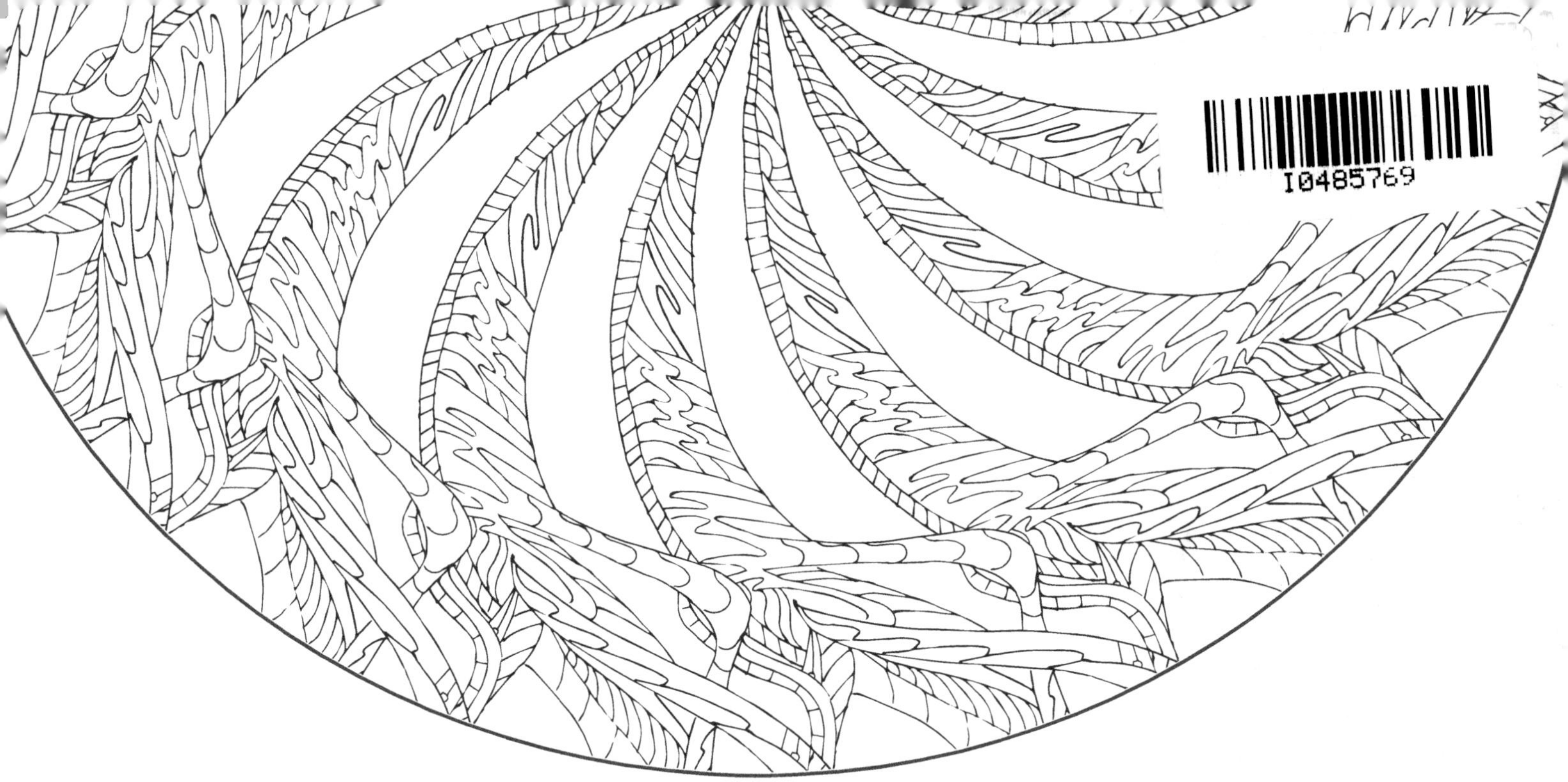

I0485769

WELCOME TO

Elements

VOLUME ONE

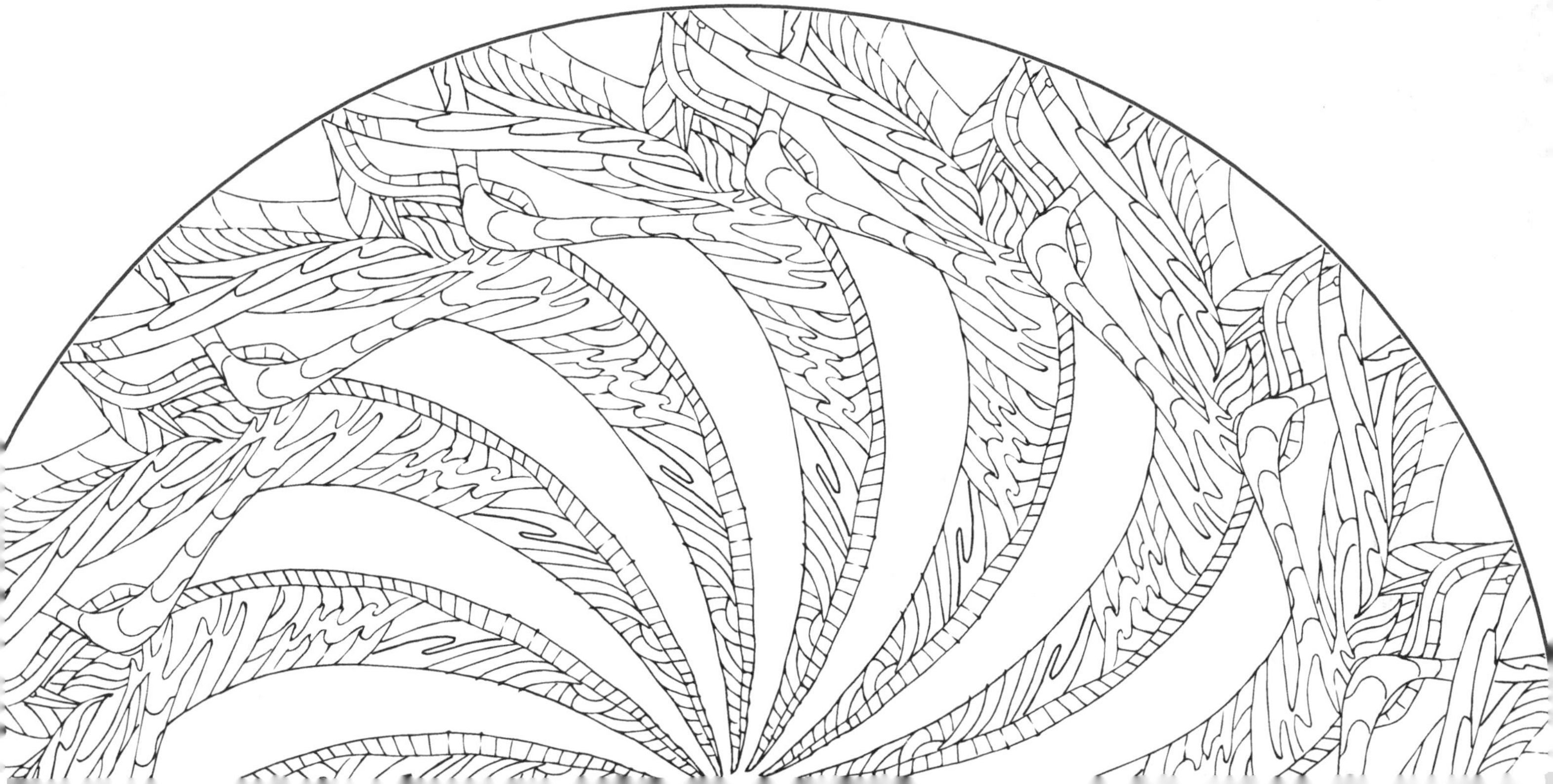

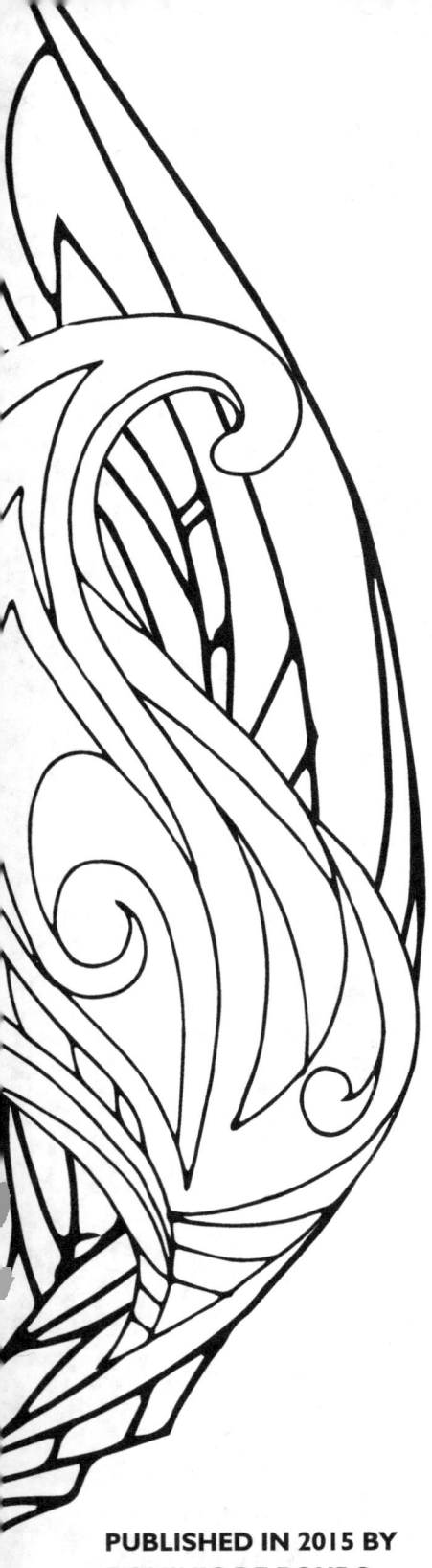

PUBLISHED IN 2015 BY
DOMINIC DE BOURG

ALL RIGHTS RESERVED, NO PART OF THIS PUBLICATION
MAY BE REPRODUCED OR TRANSMITTED IN ANY FORM
OR BY ANY MEANS, ELECTRONIC OR MECHANICAL,
INCLUDING PHOTOCOPY, RECORDING OR ANY INFORMATION
STORAGE AND RETRIEVAL SYSTEM, WITHOUT PERMISSION
IN WRITING FROM THE ARTIST AND PUBLISHER.

ALL ARTWORK CREATED BY DOMINIC DE BOURG

Hey there,
Thanks for picking up this book!

In here you'll find a collection of abstract flowers and animals for you to colour, using anything from crayons to paints. There's place for you to create using colour, and there's place for you to continue the designs on the page, drawing and creating patterns and designs of your own.

Do enjoy, and most importantly,
have fun!

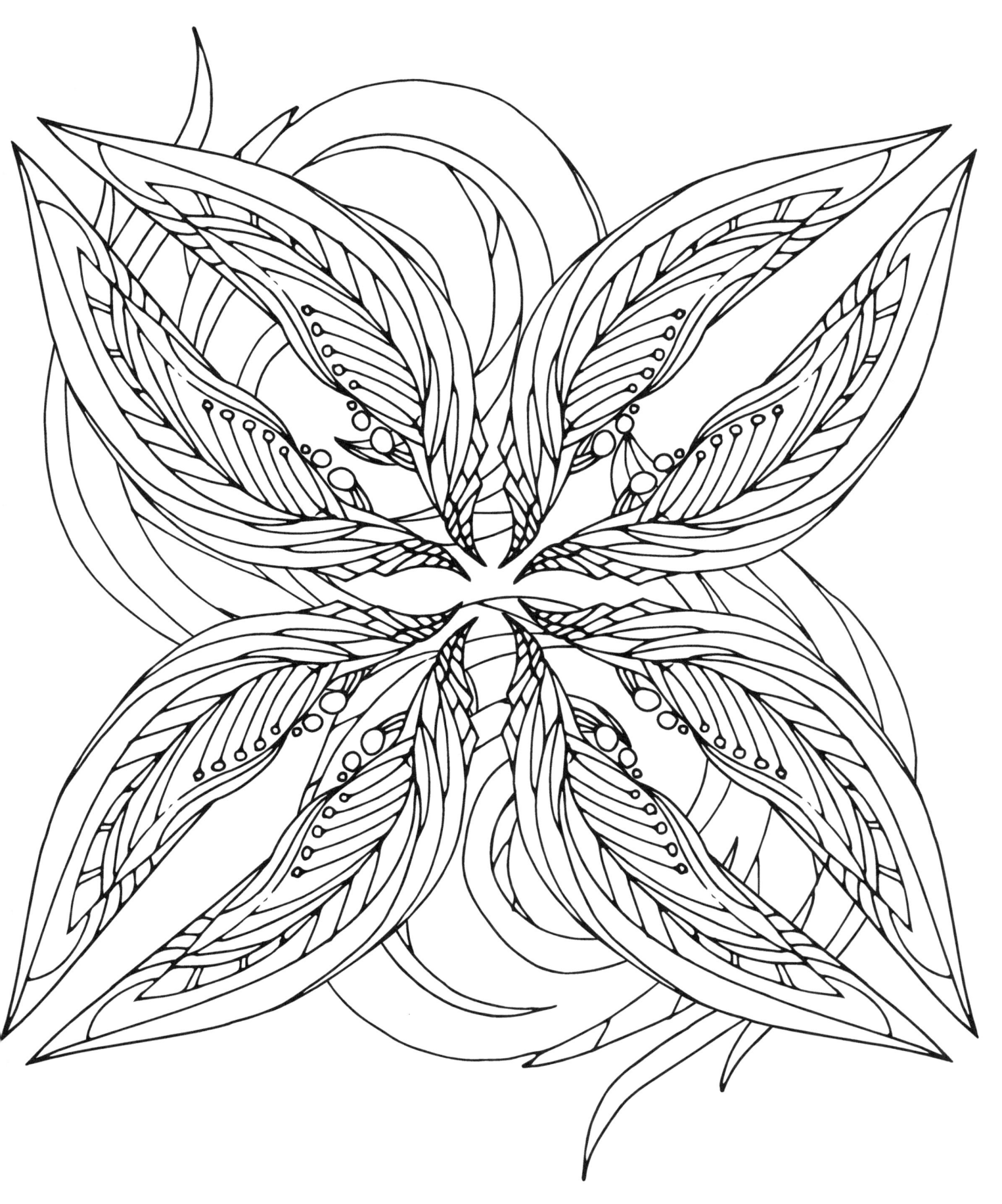

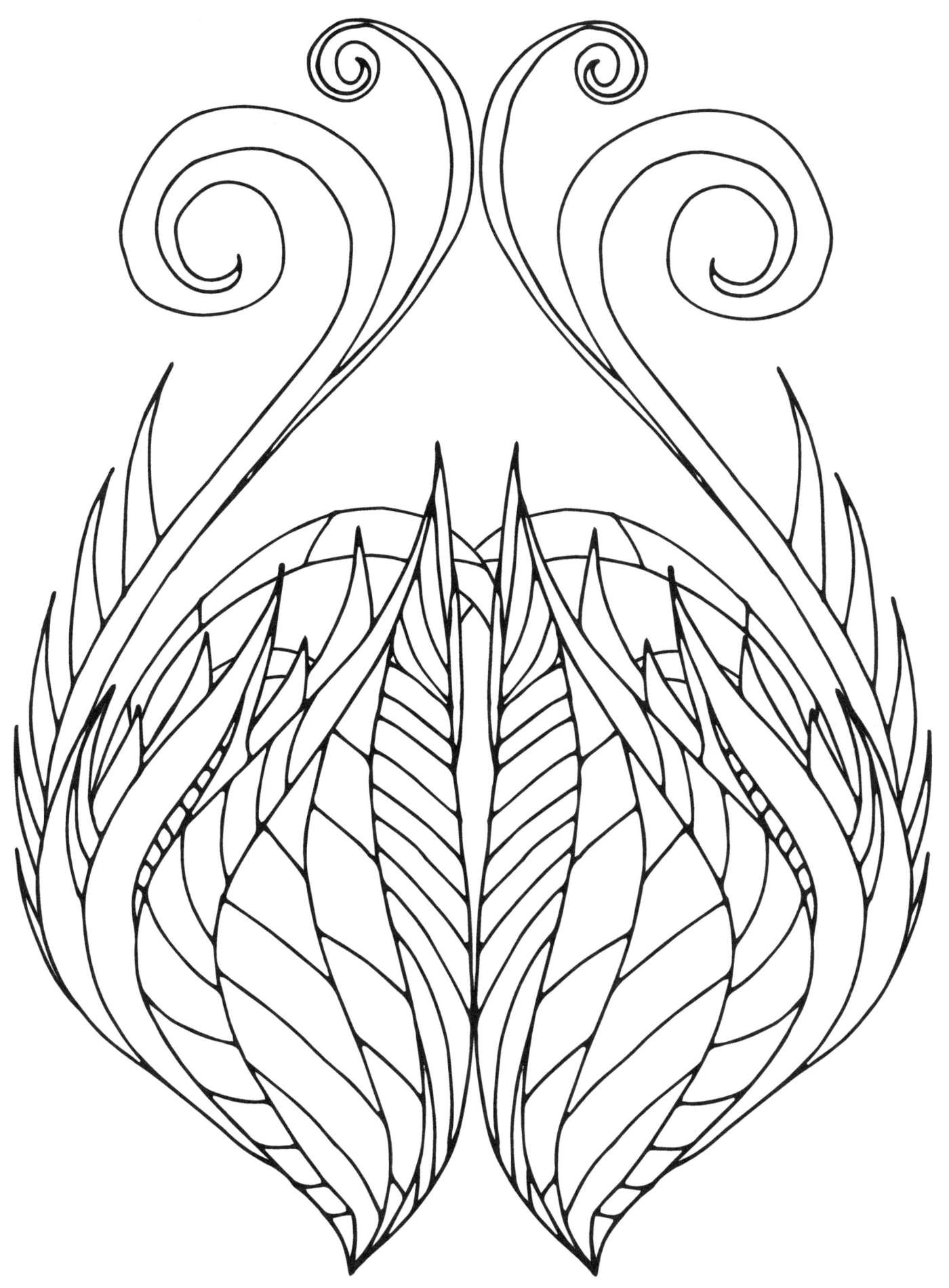

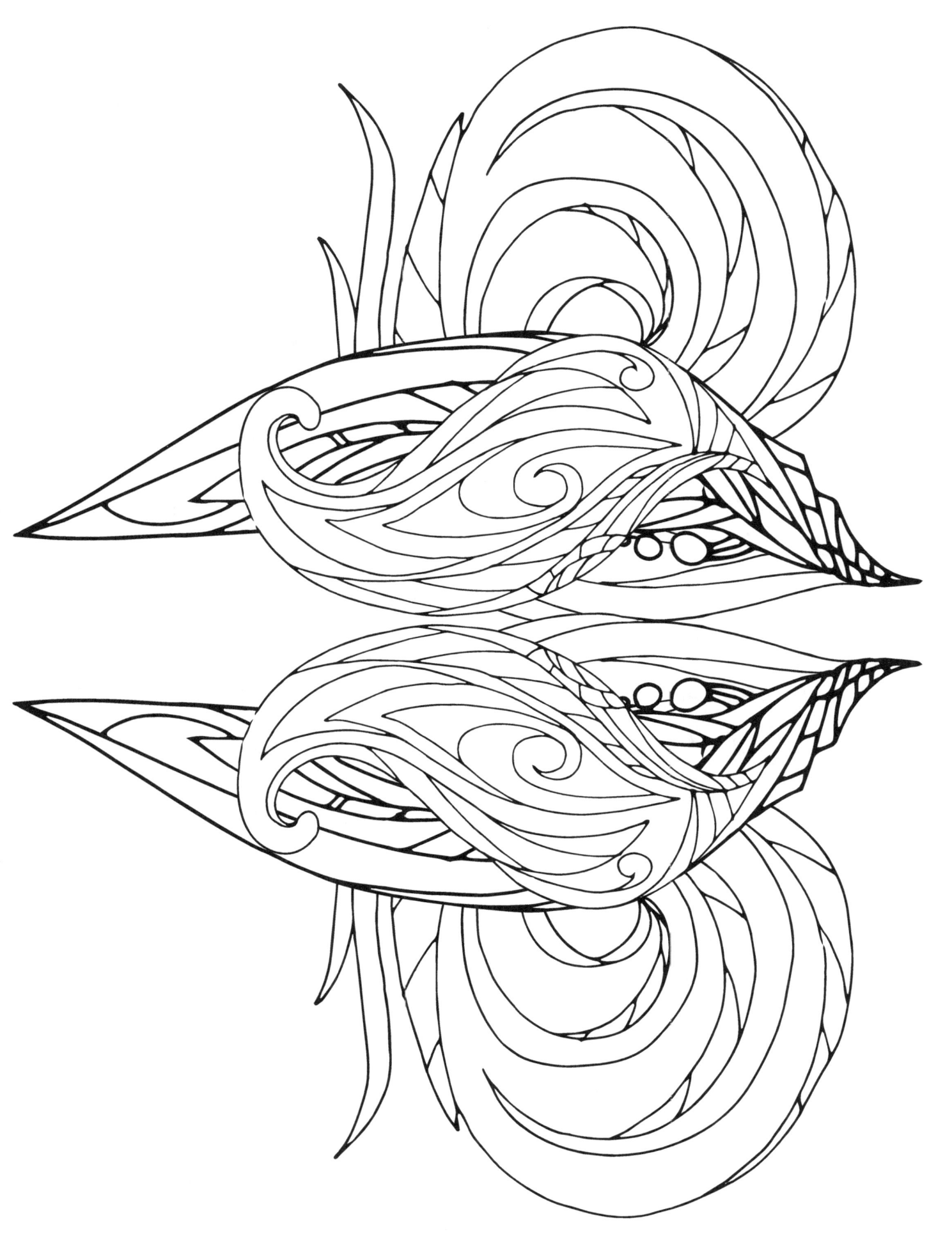

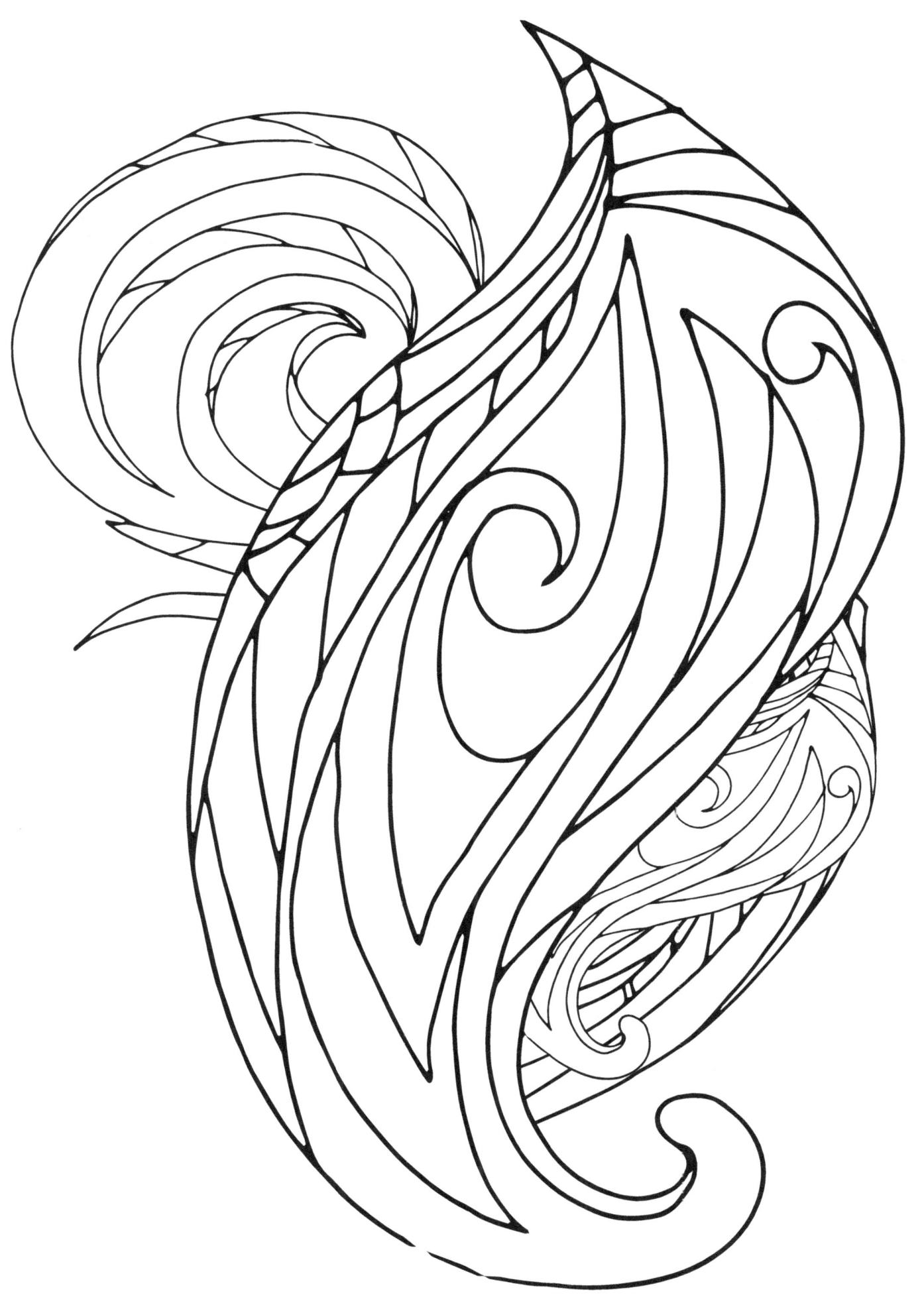

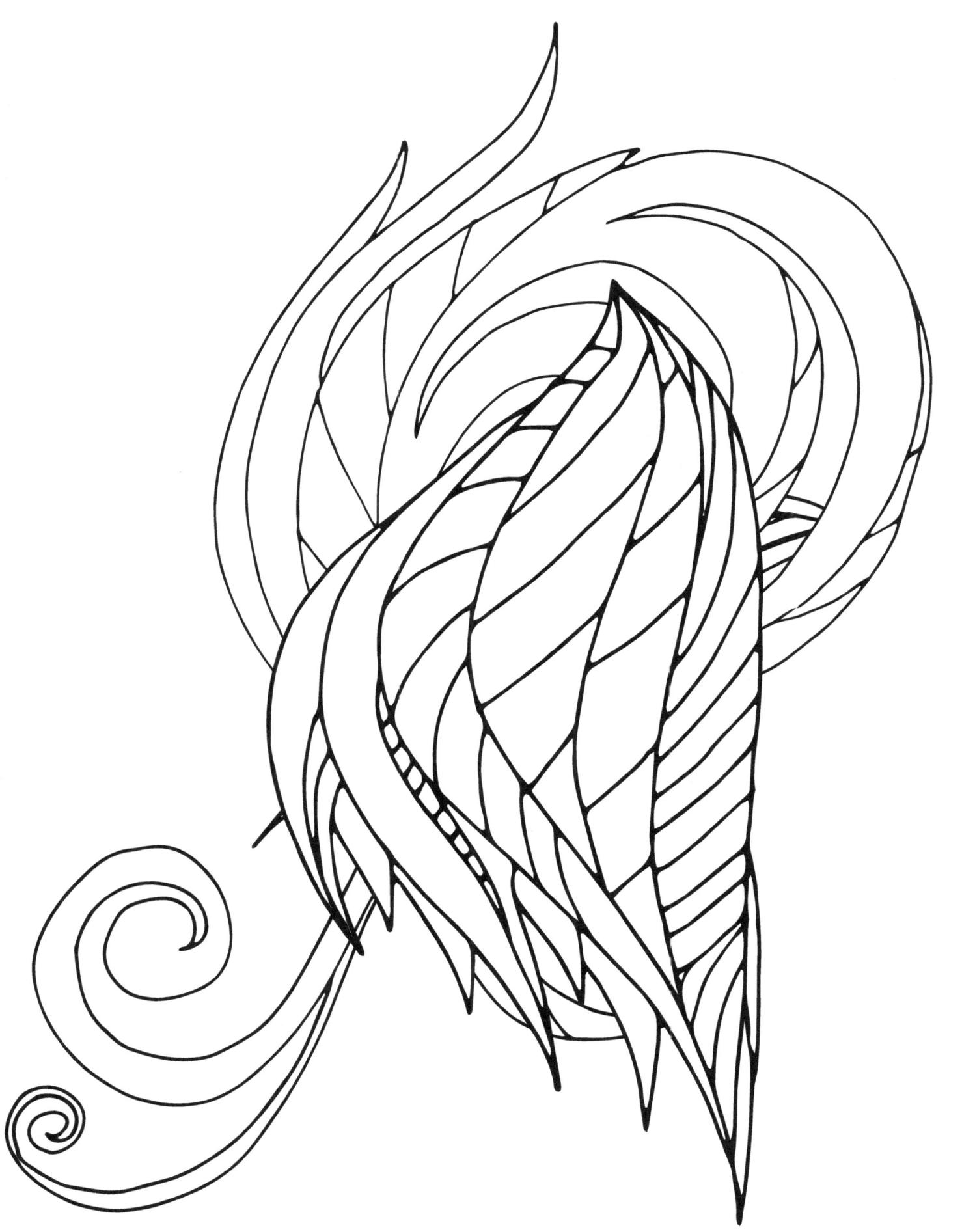

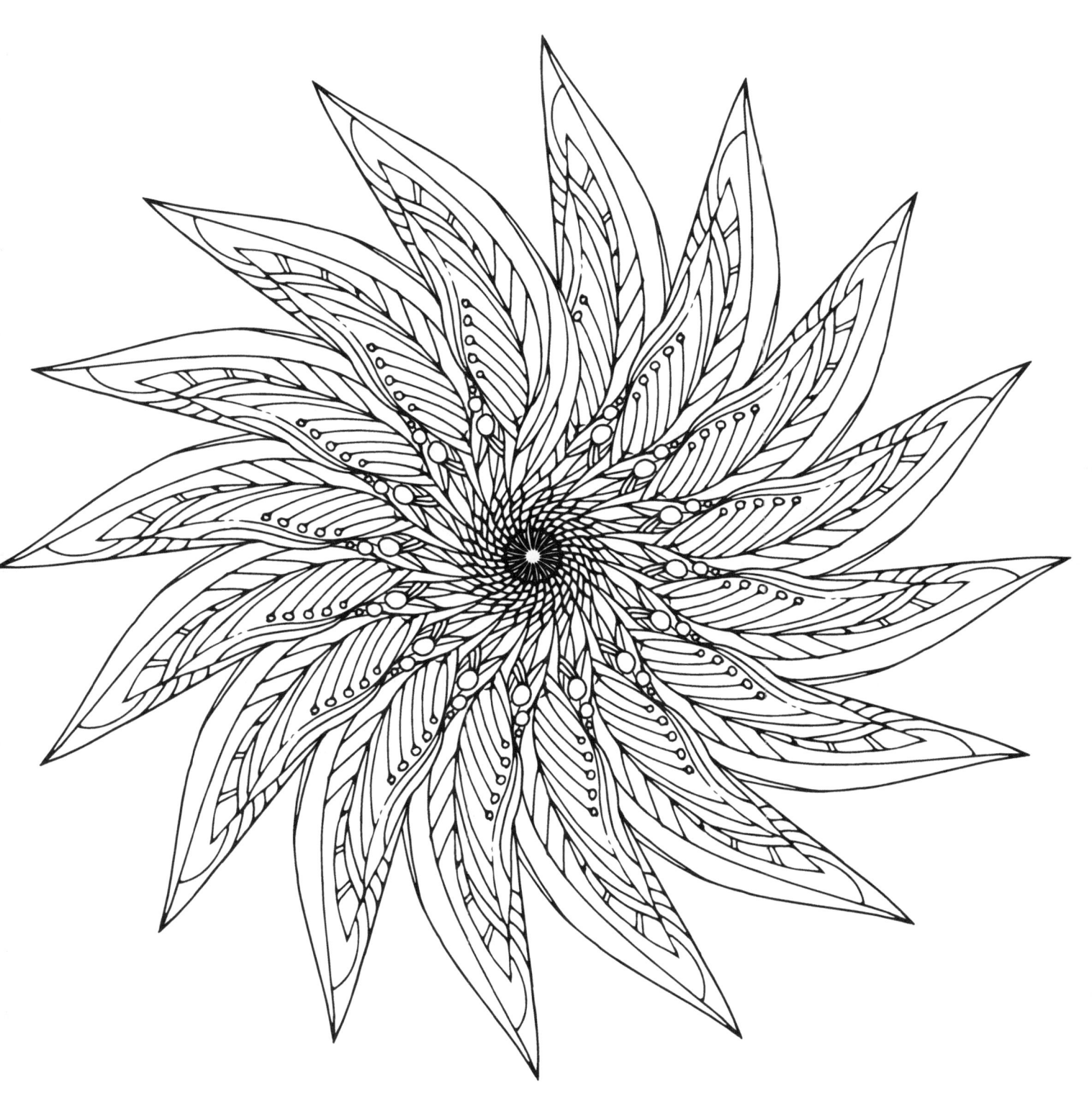

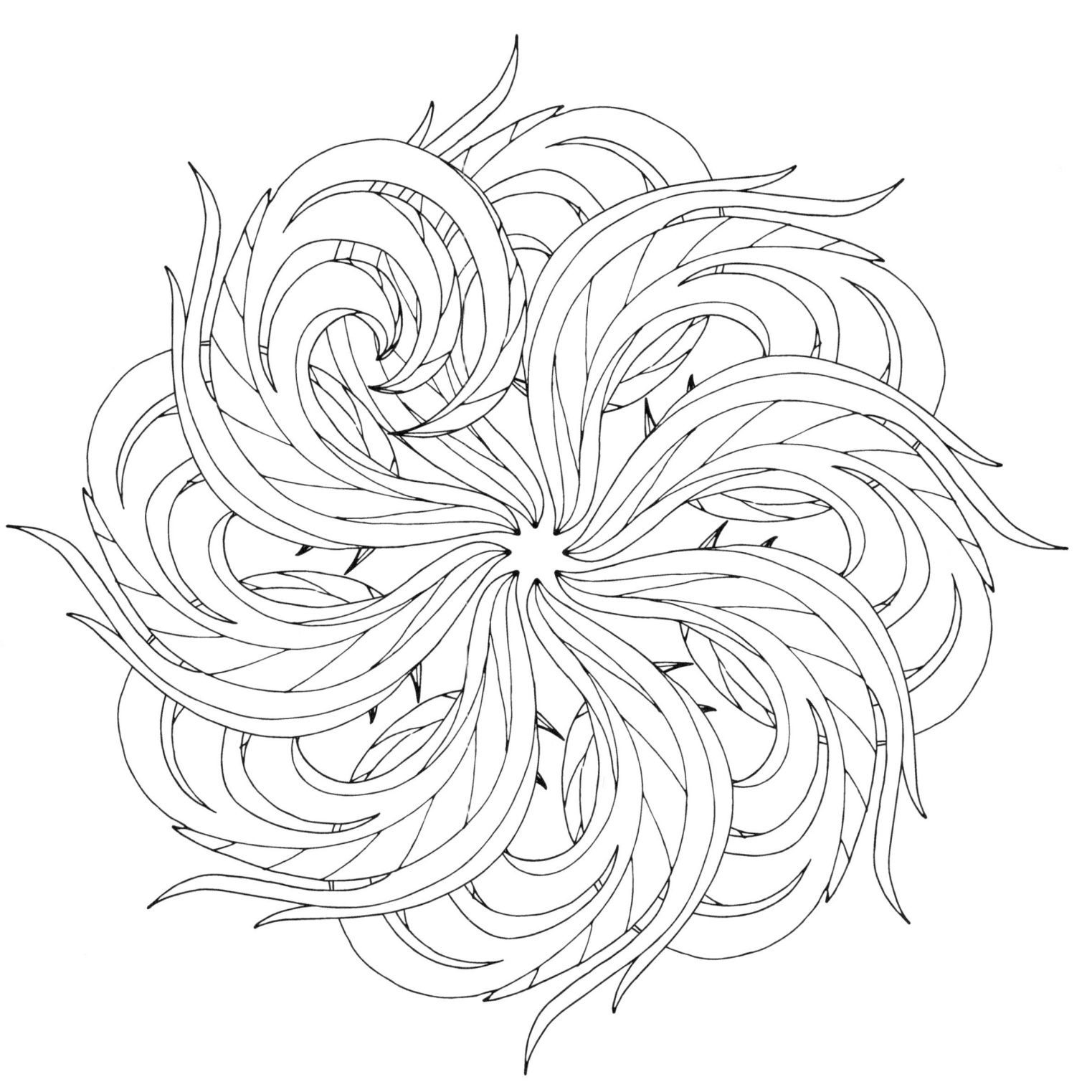

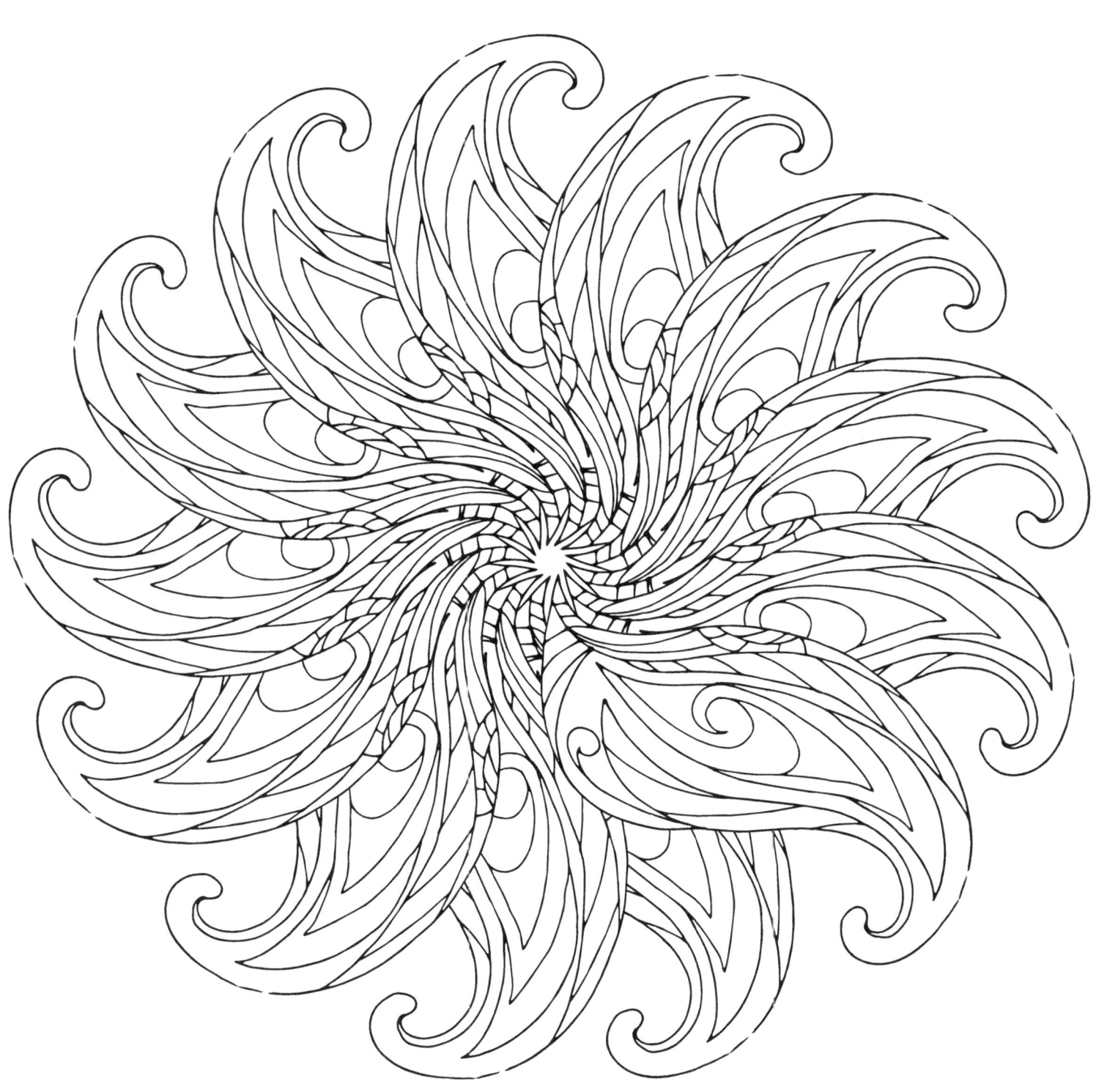

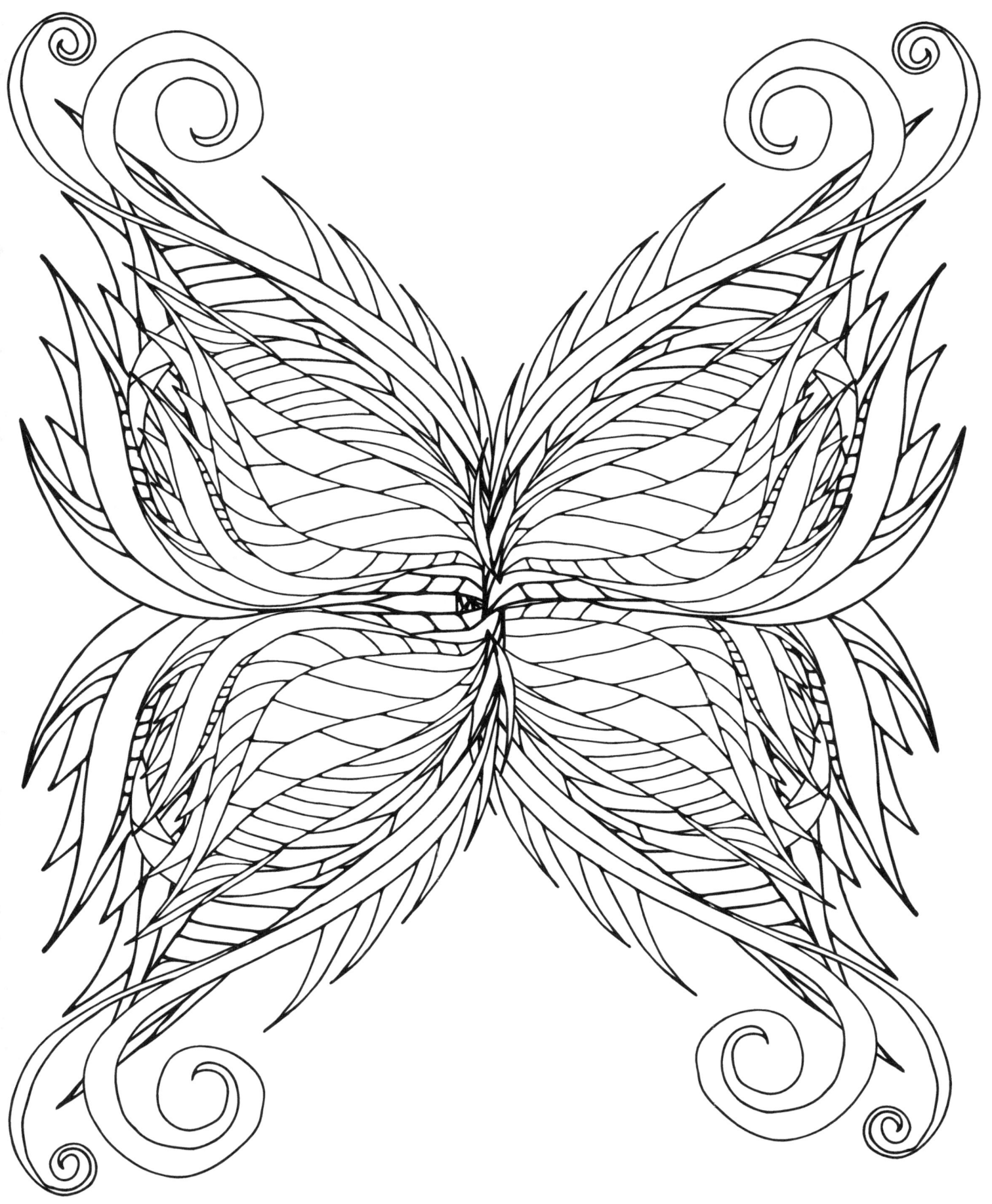

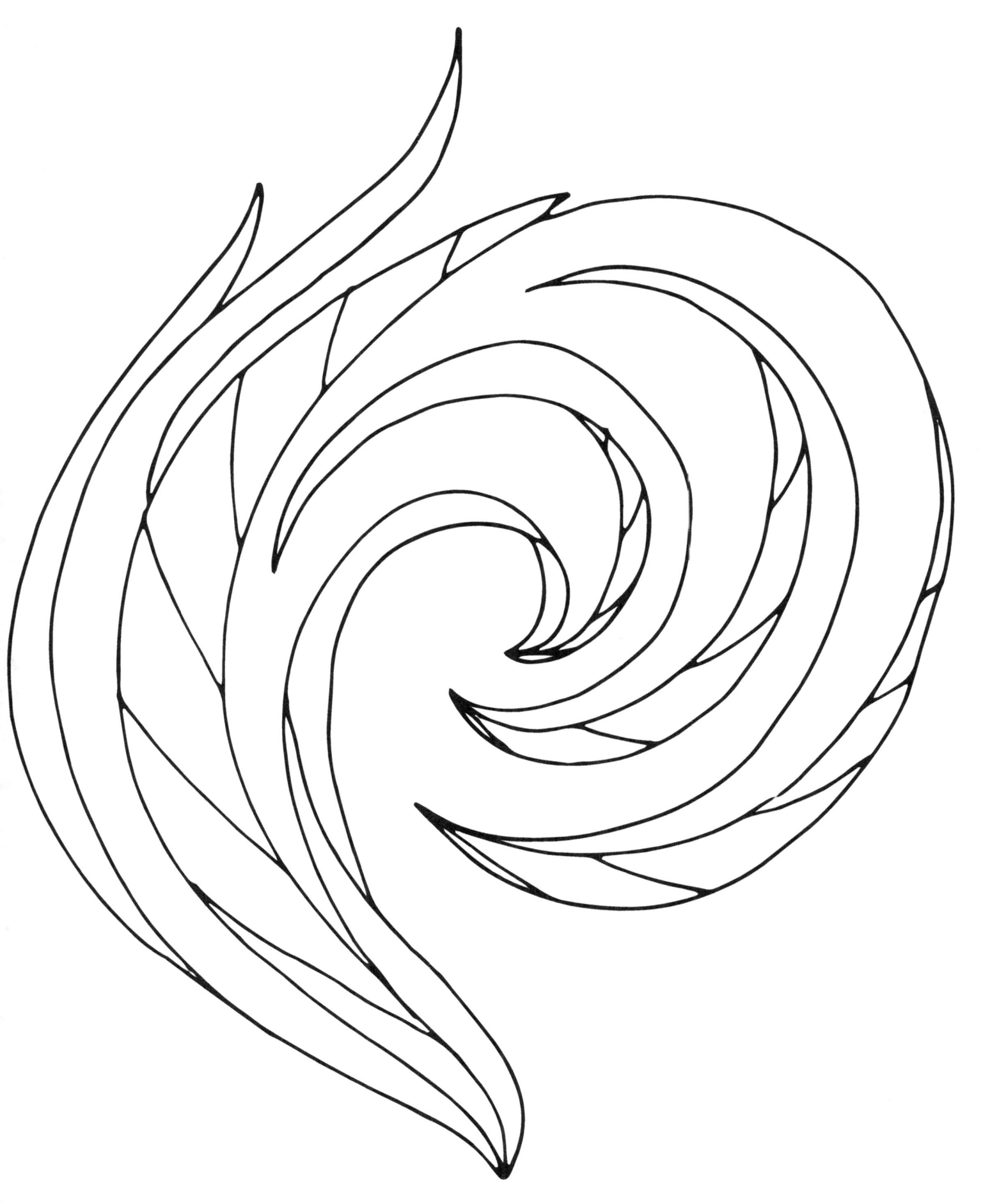

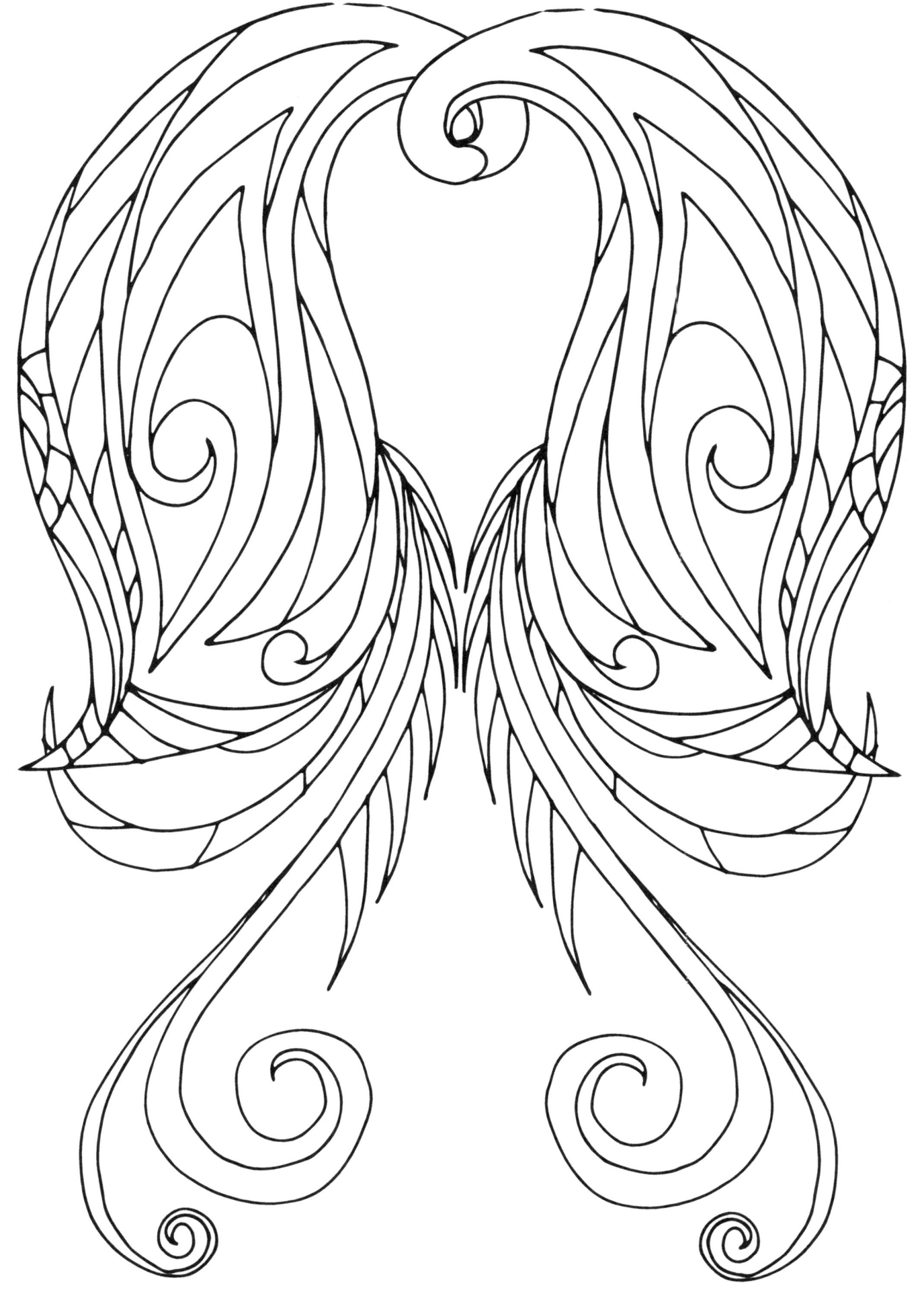

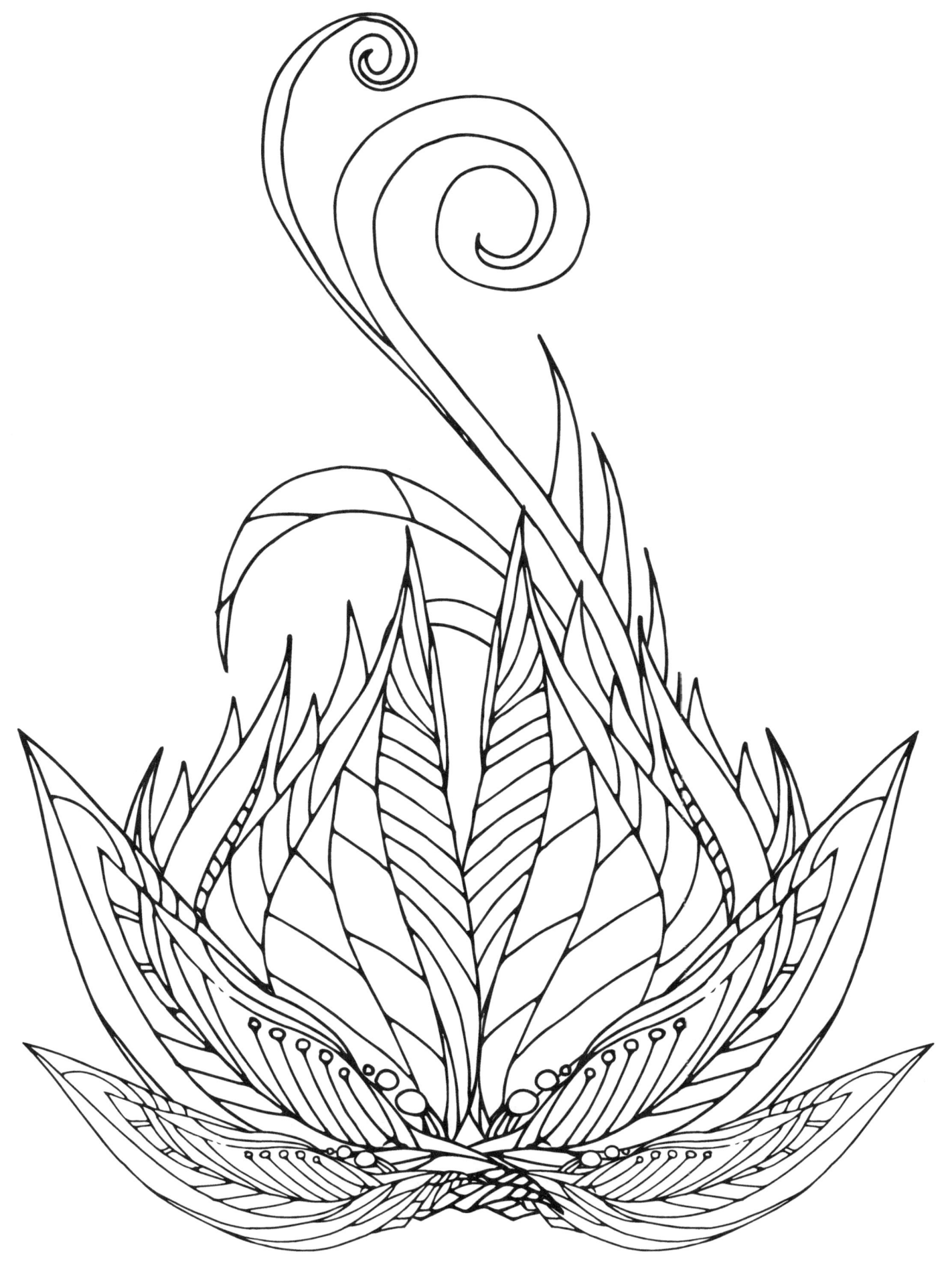

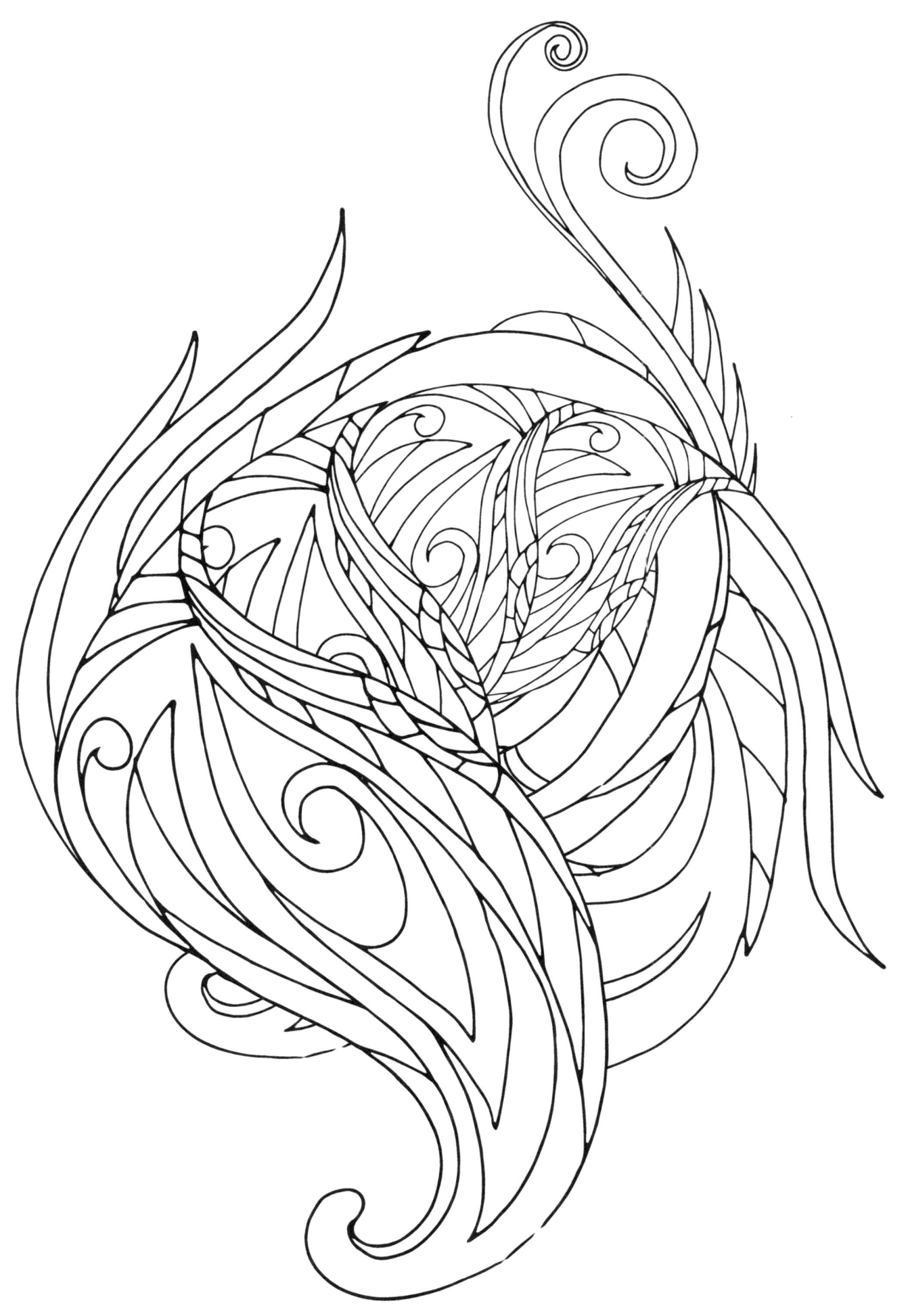

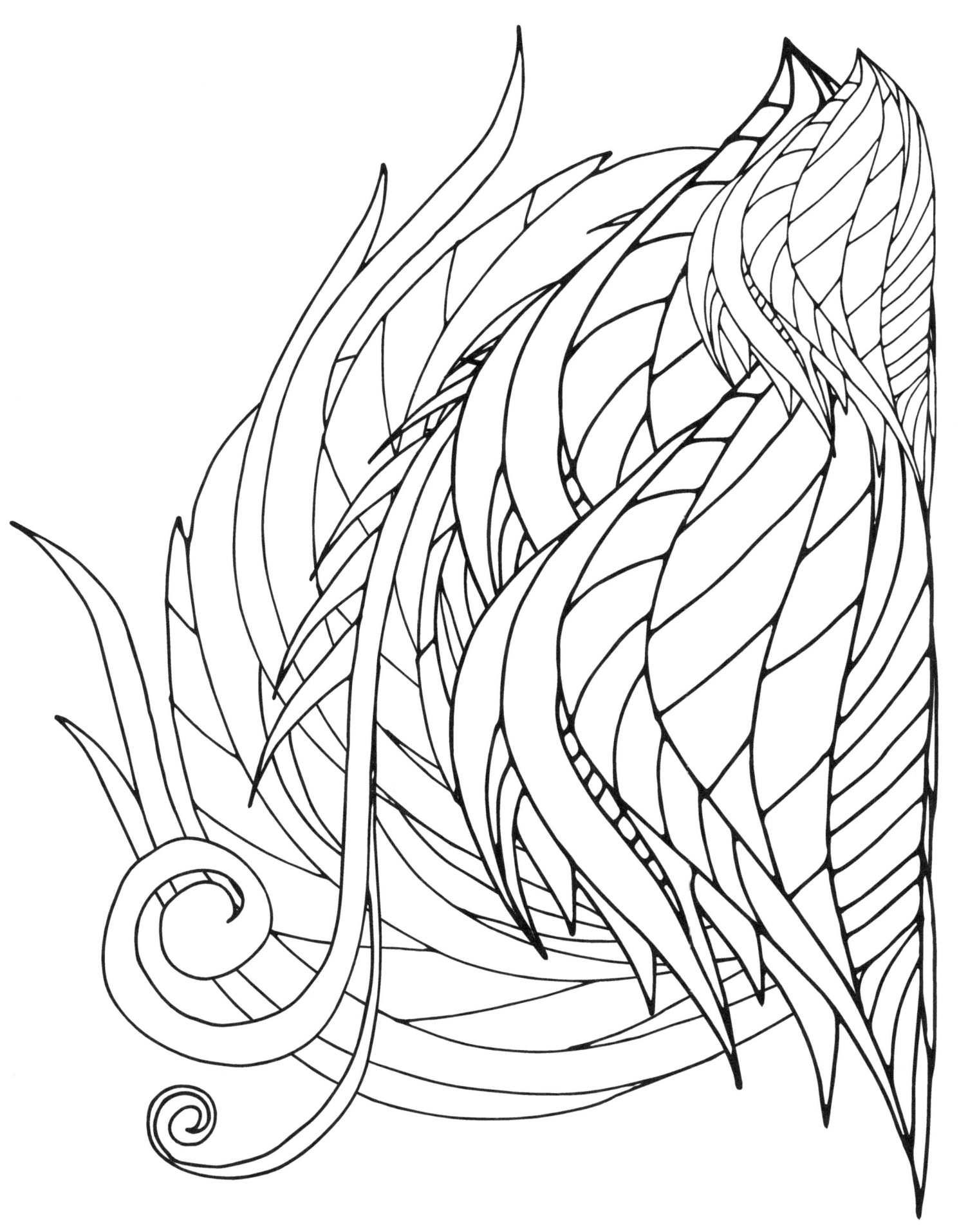

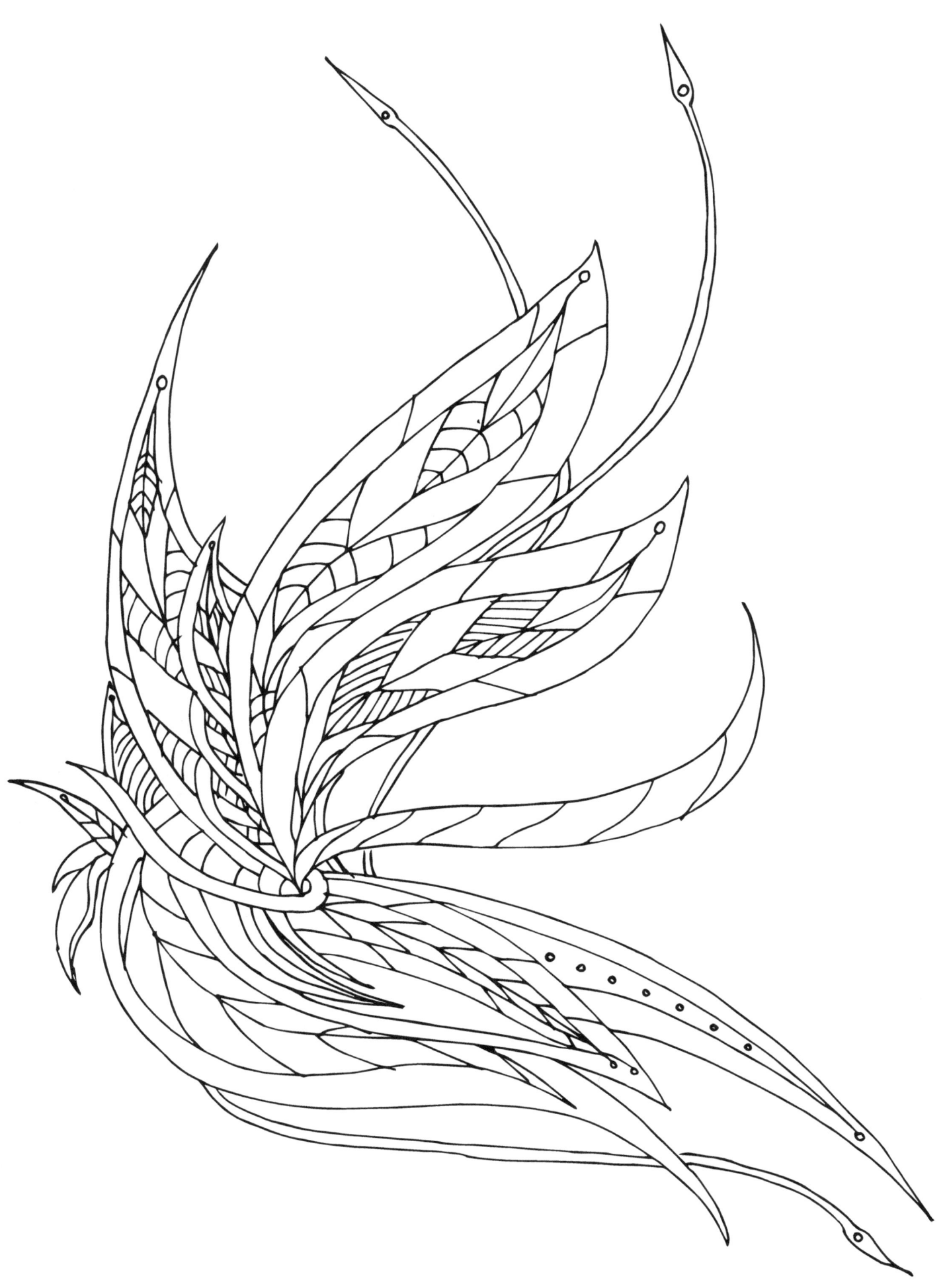

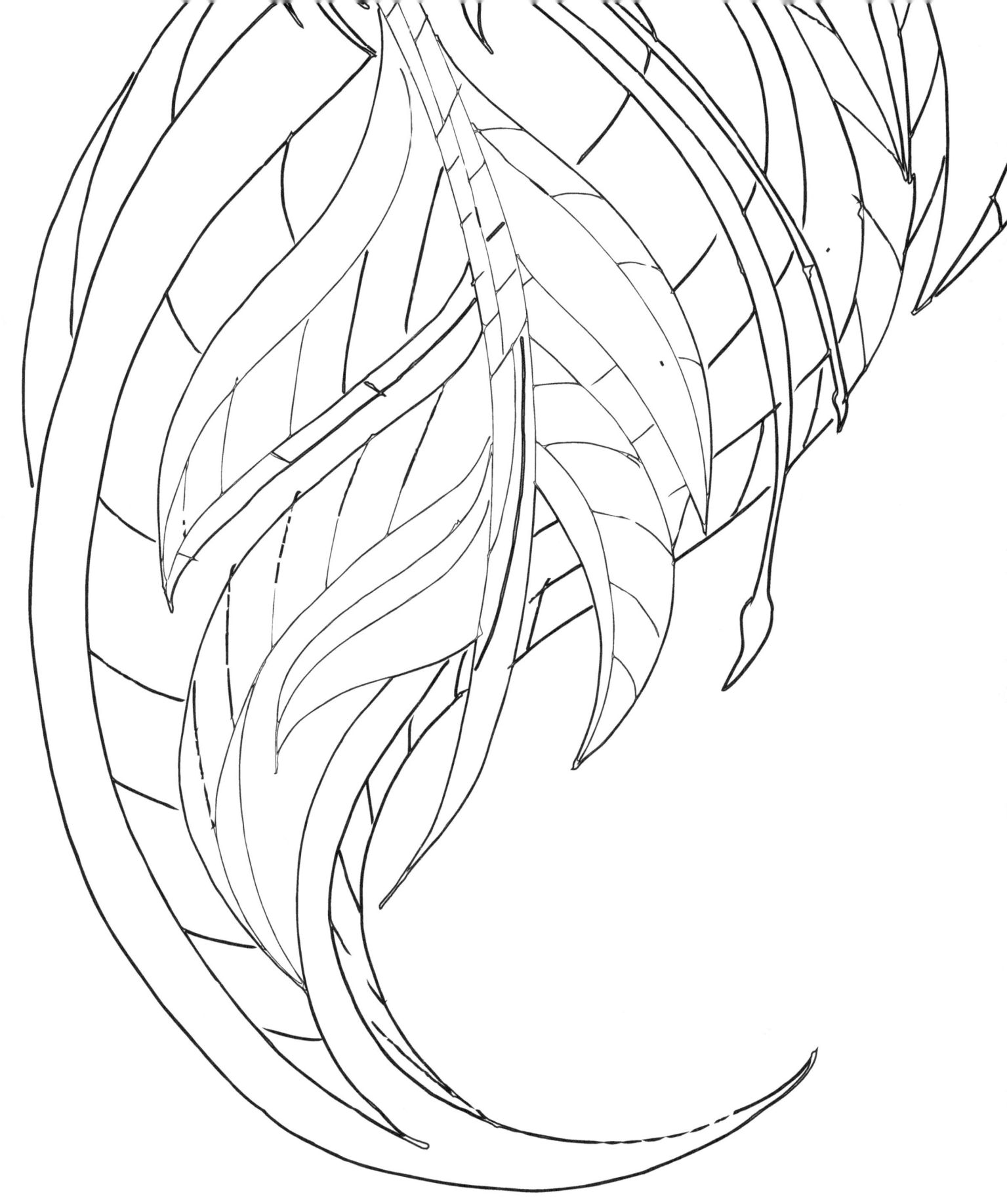

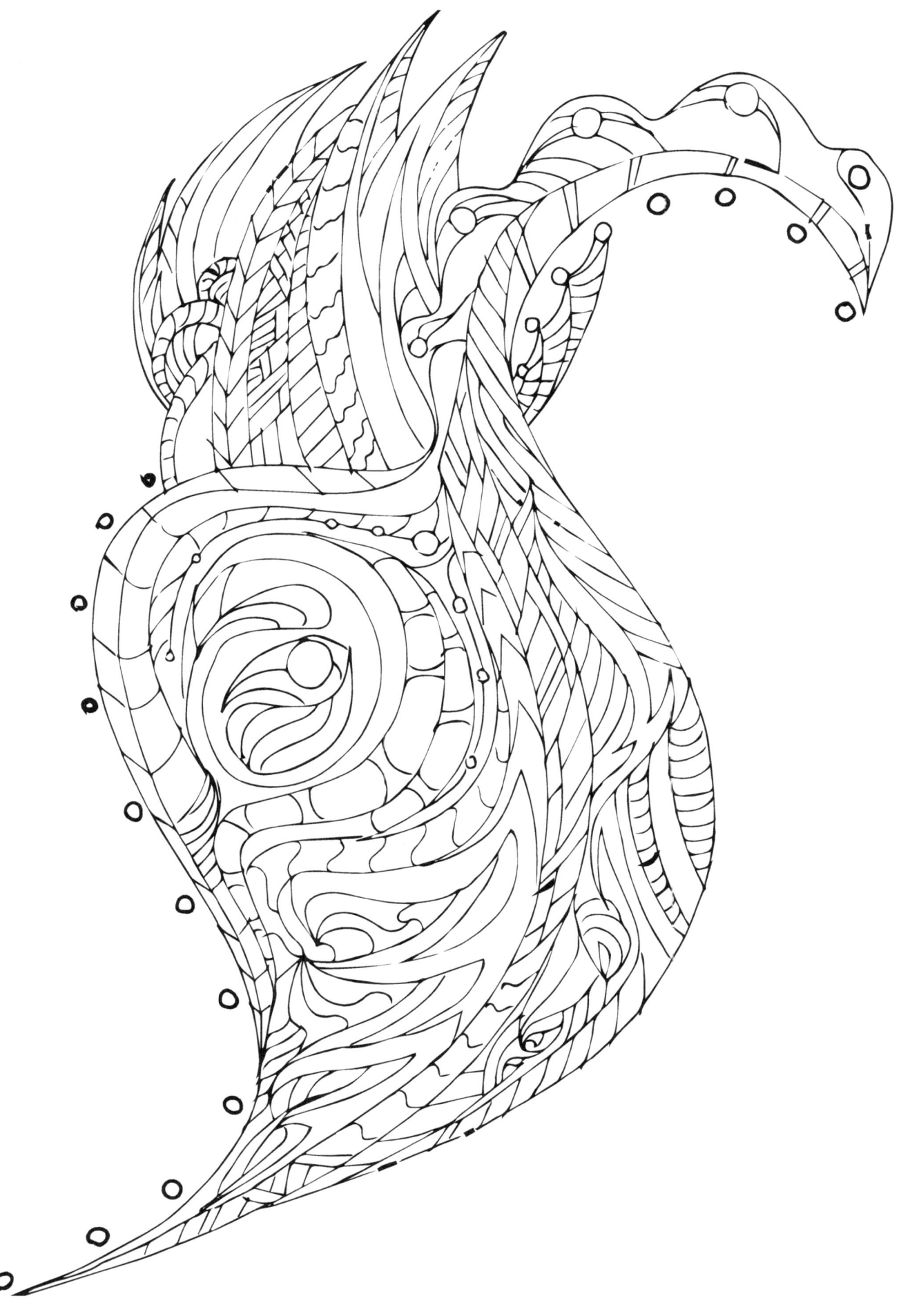

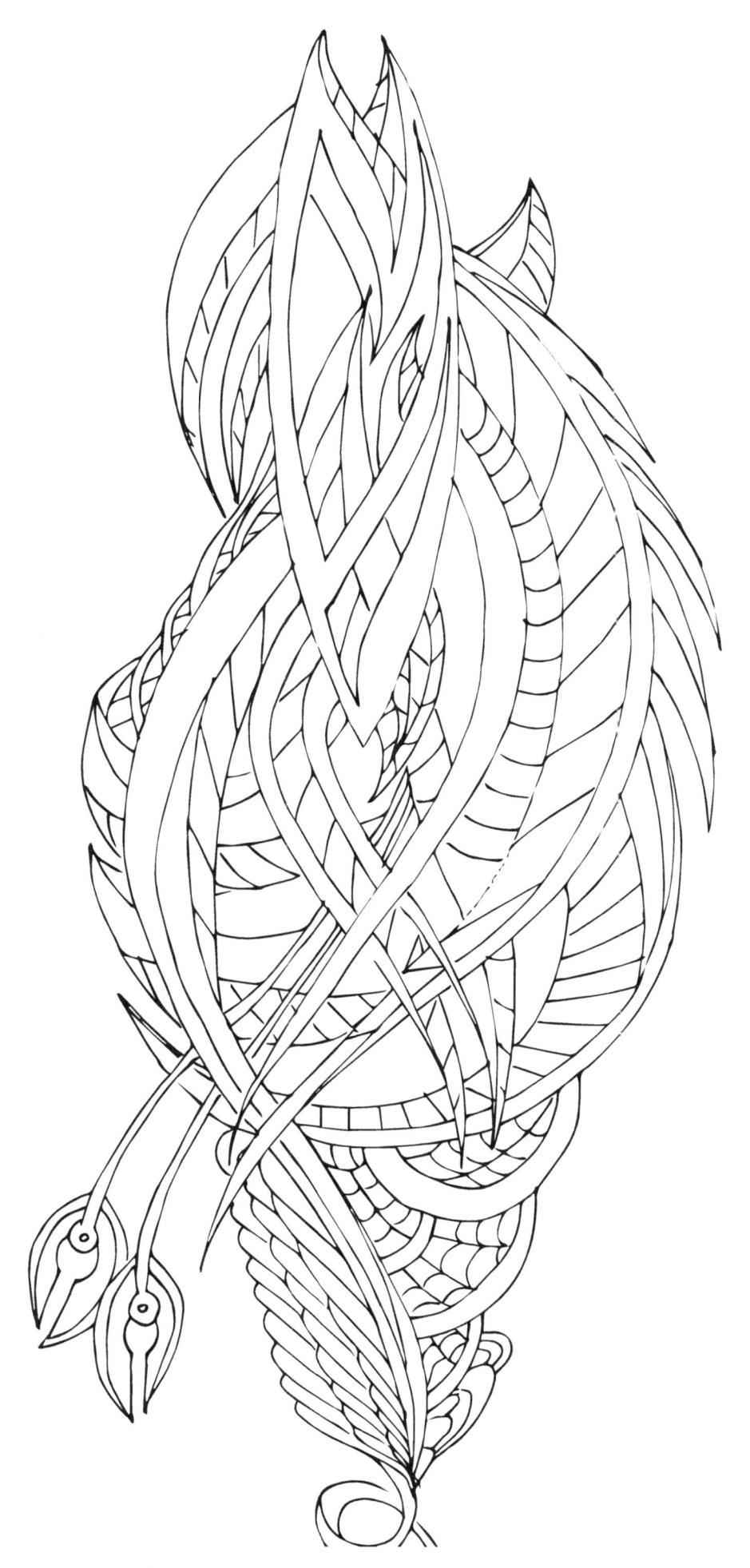

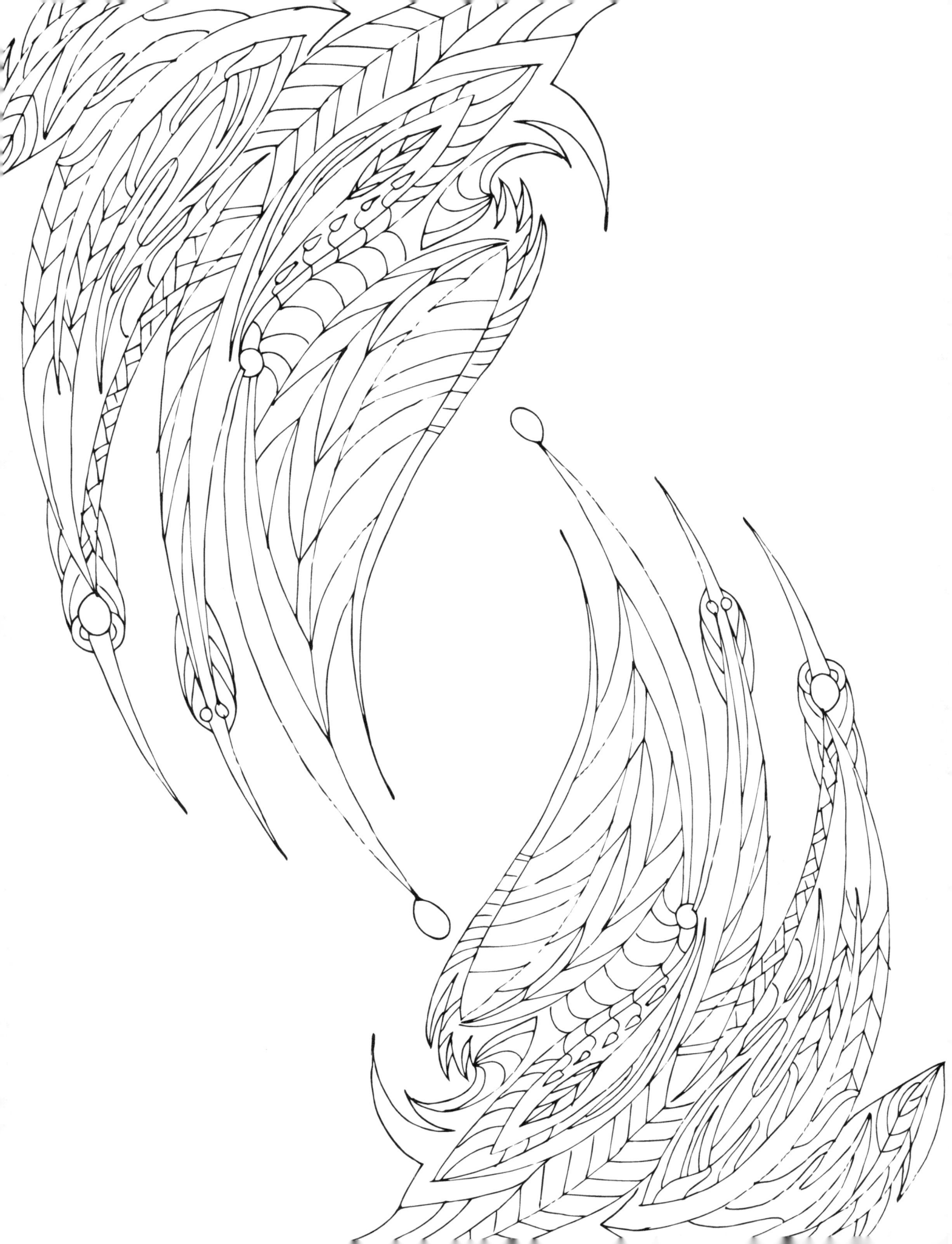

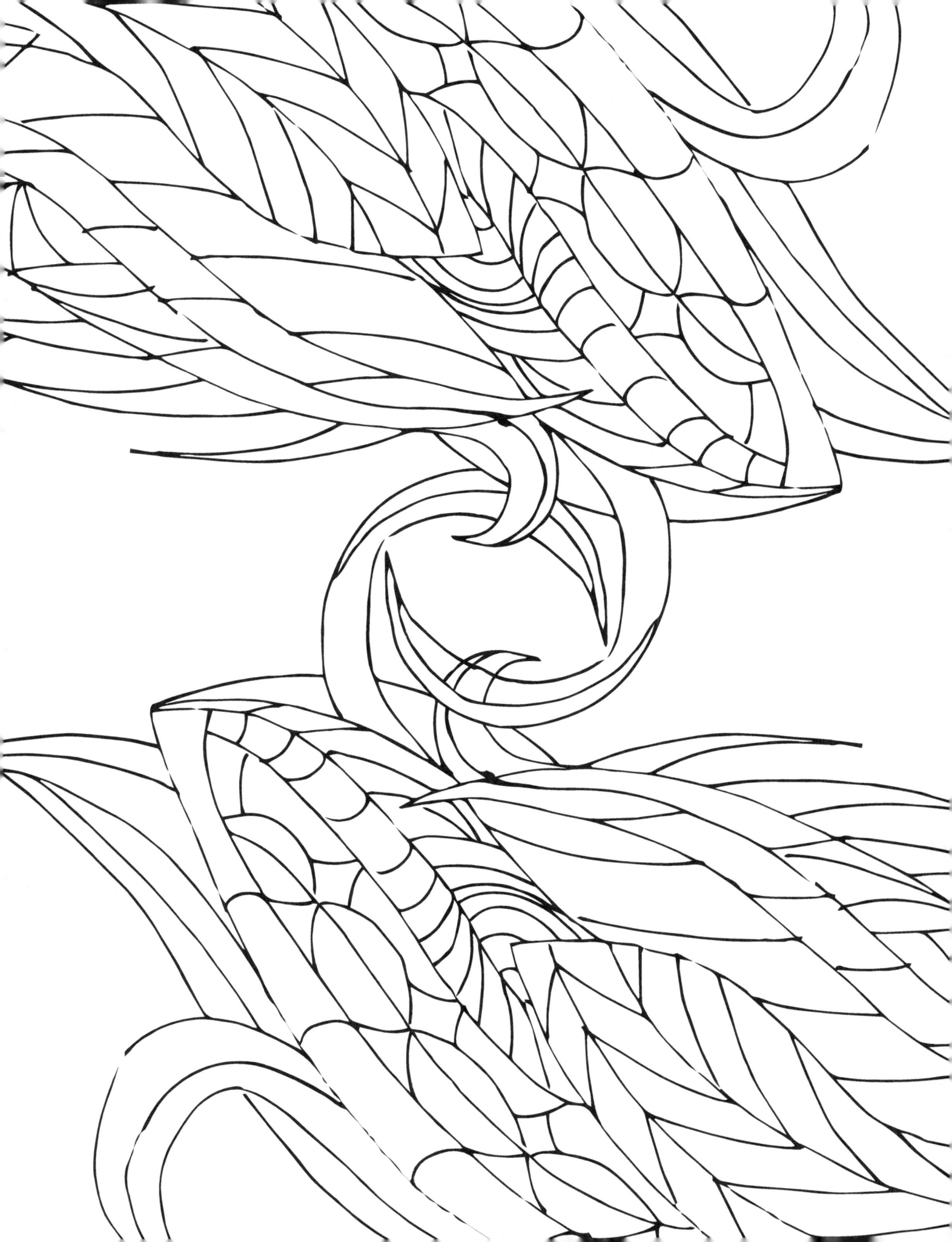

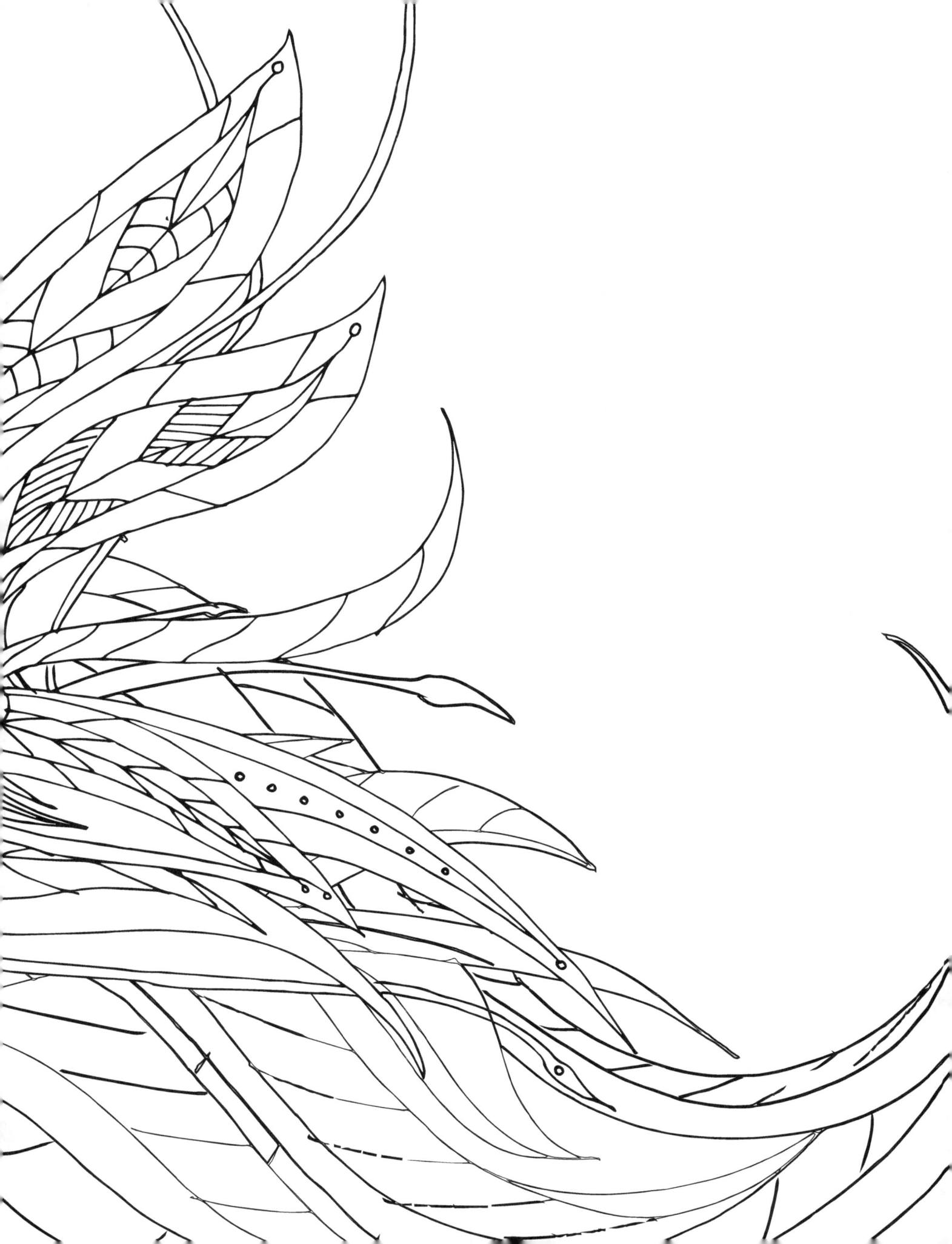

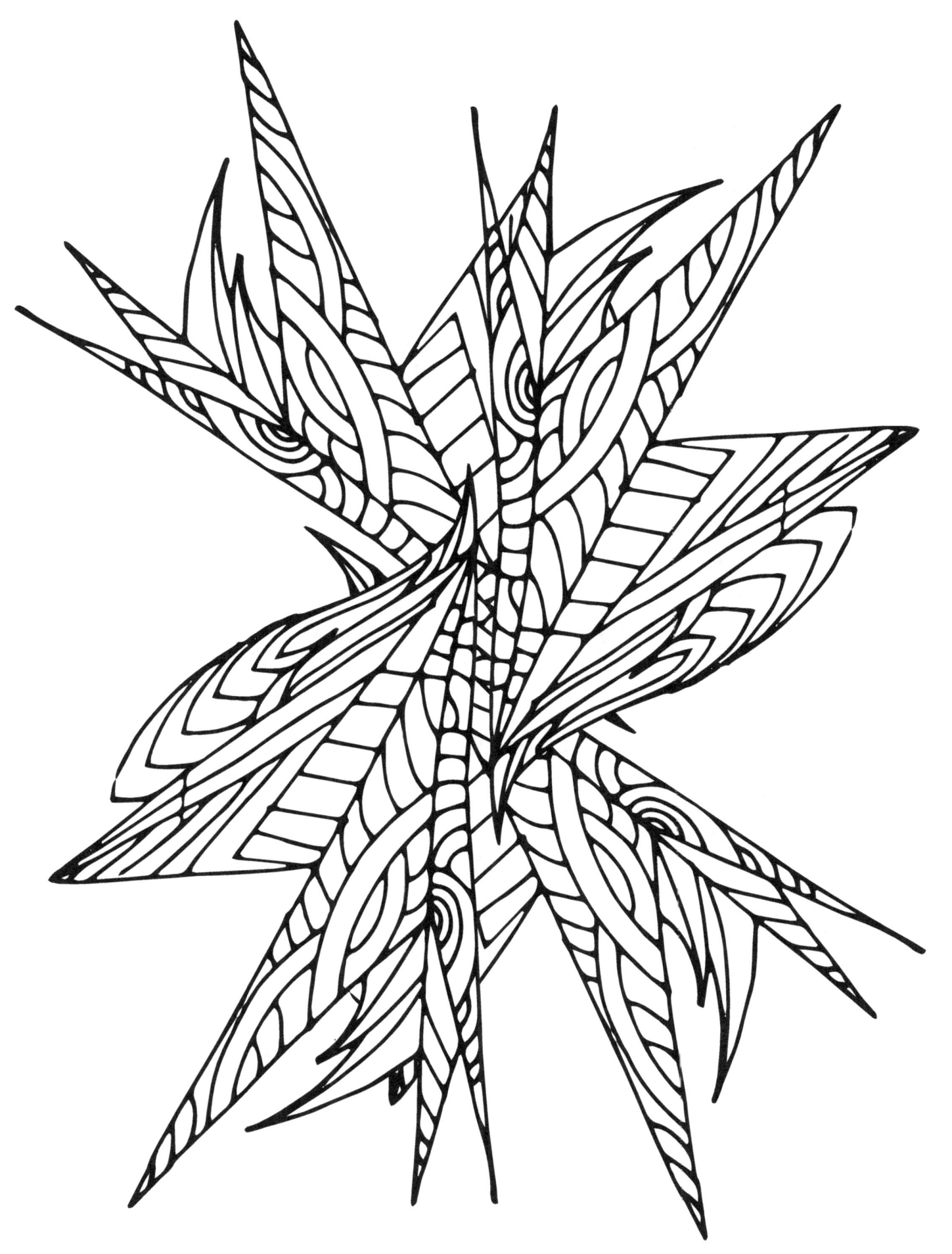

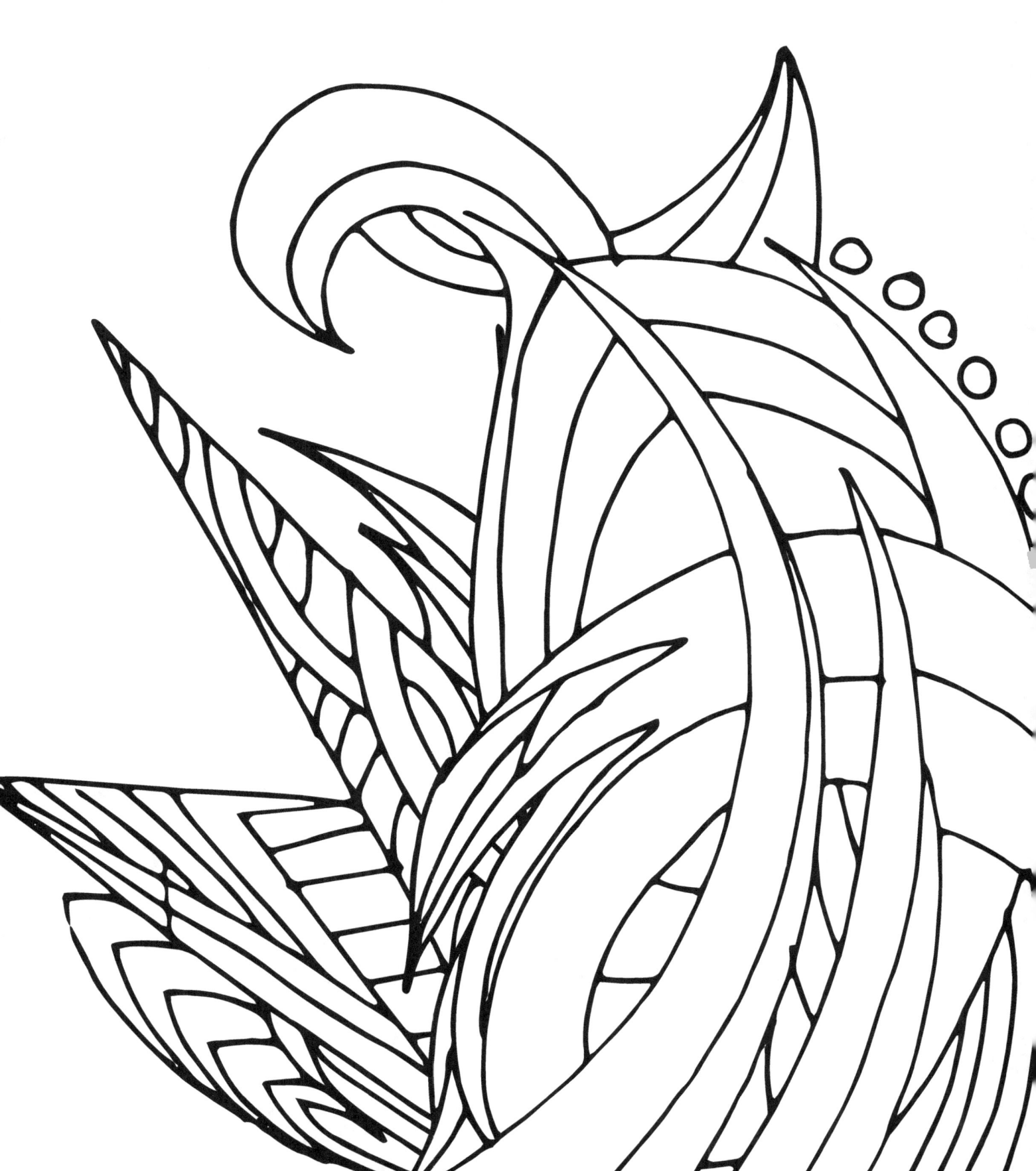

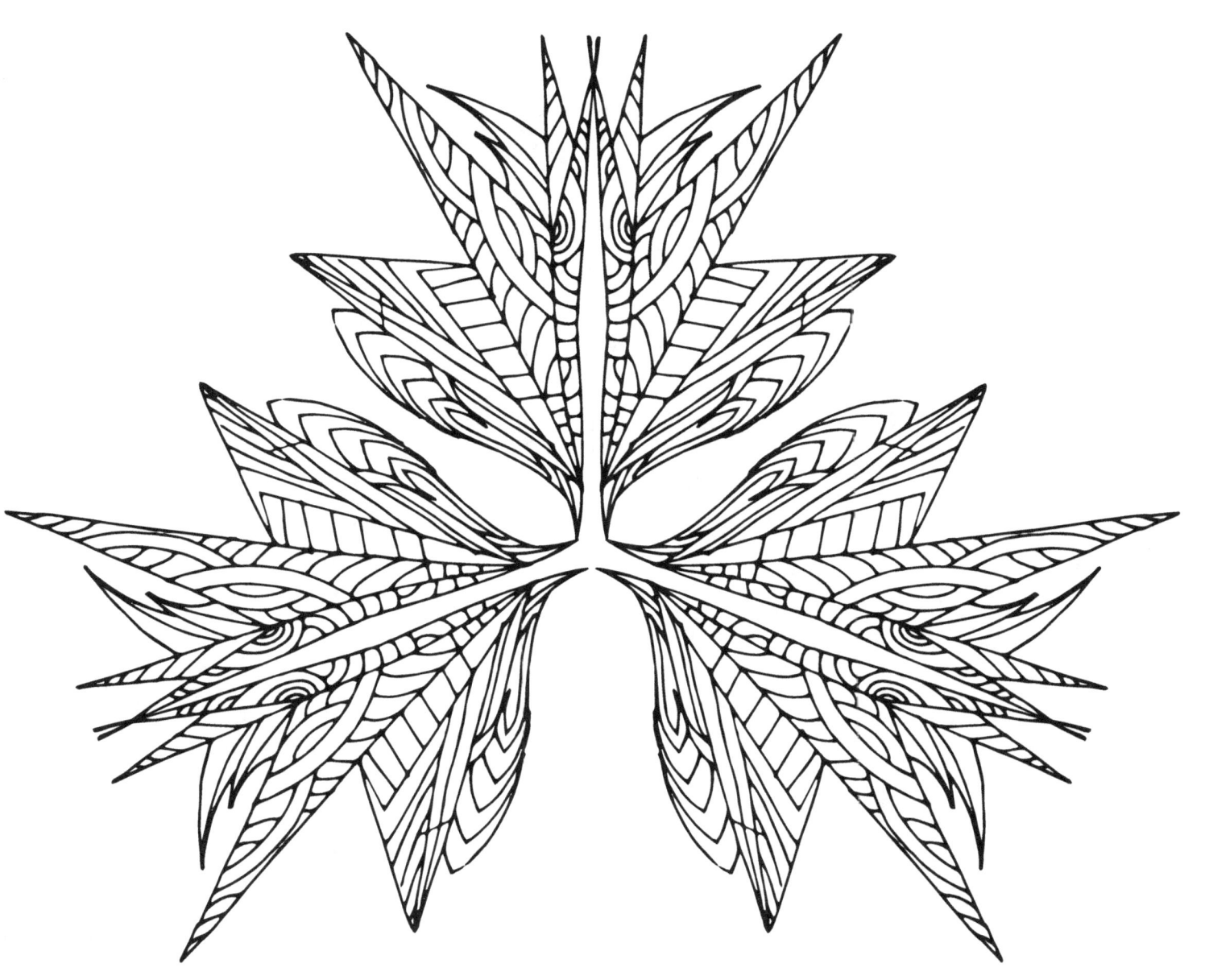

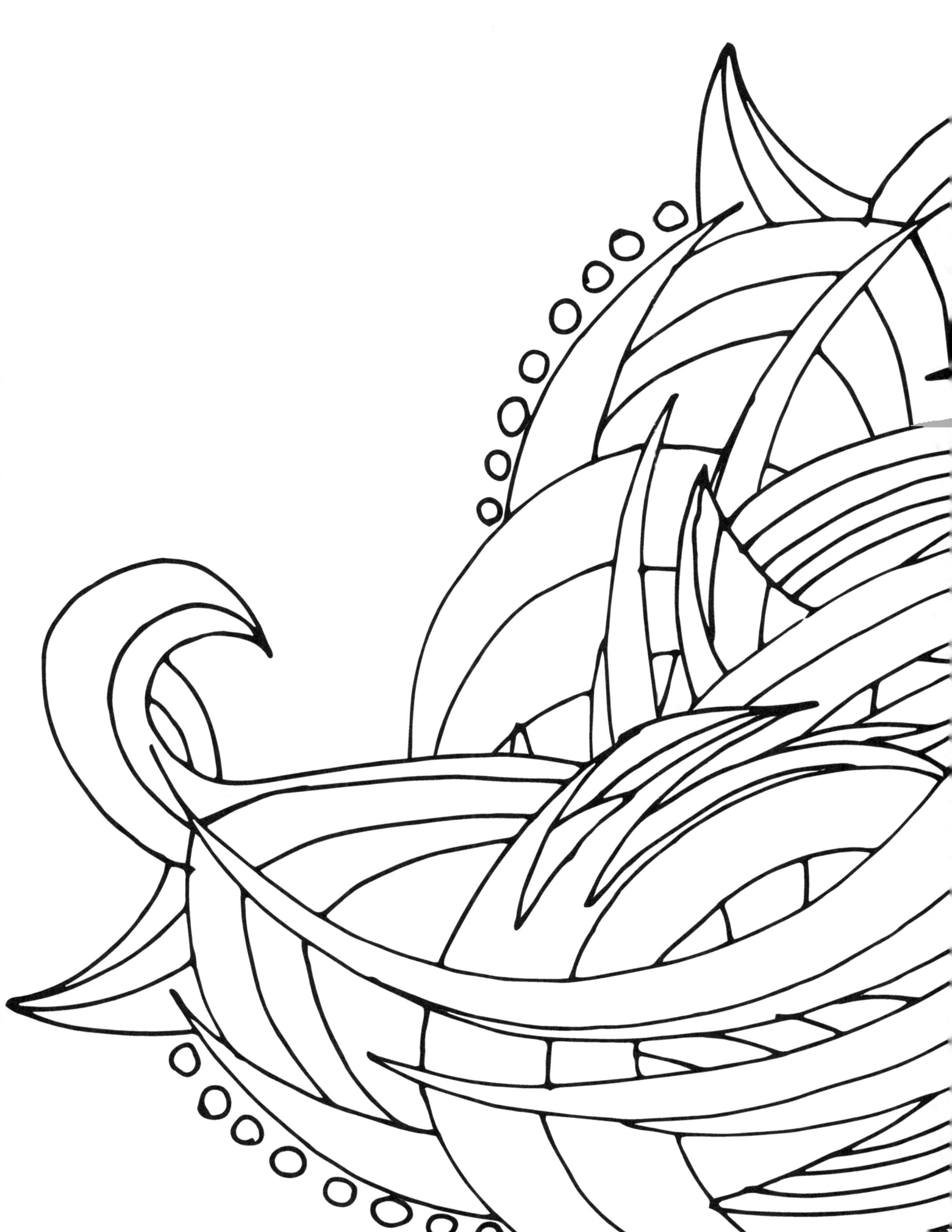

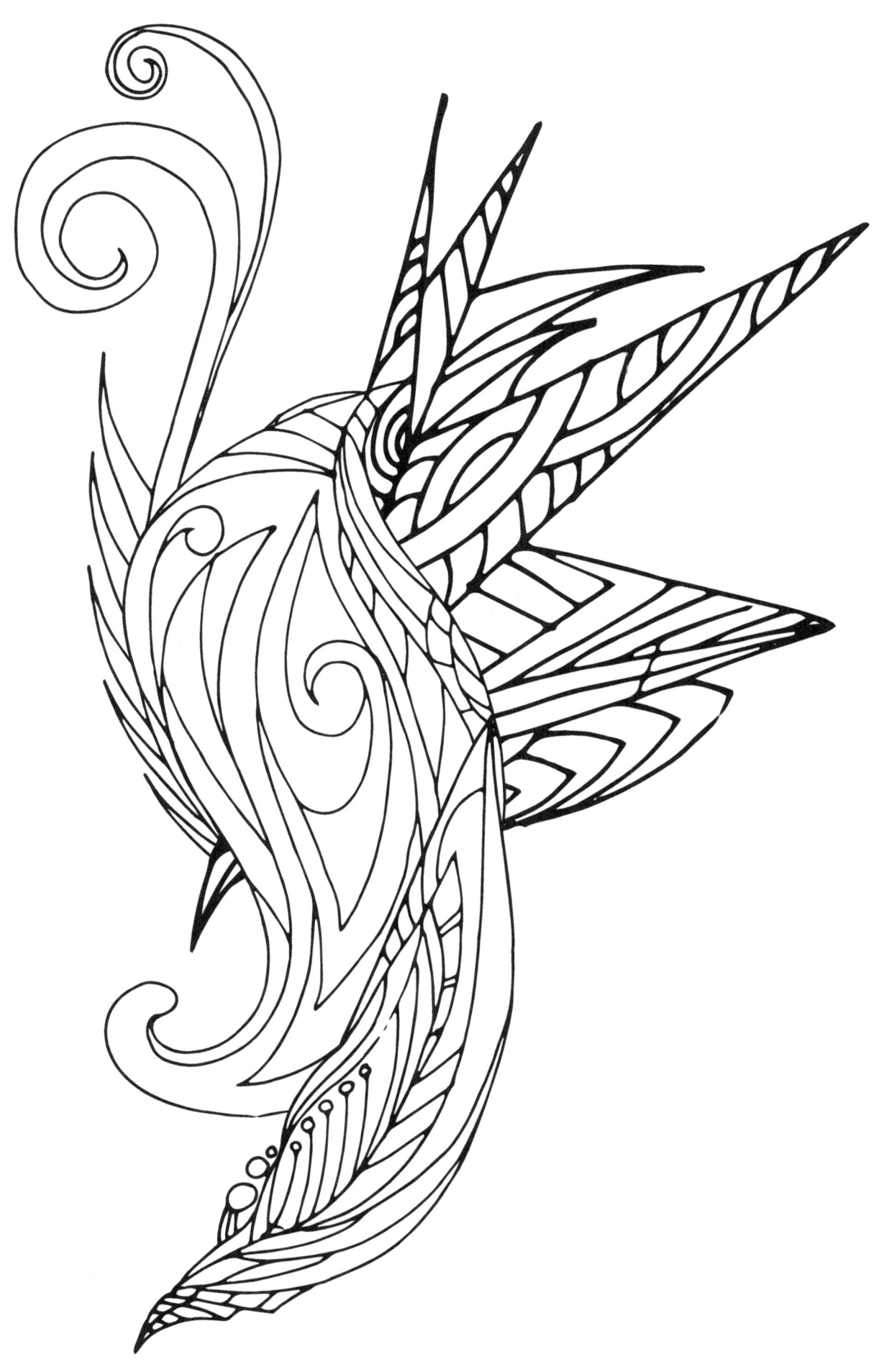

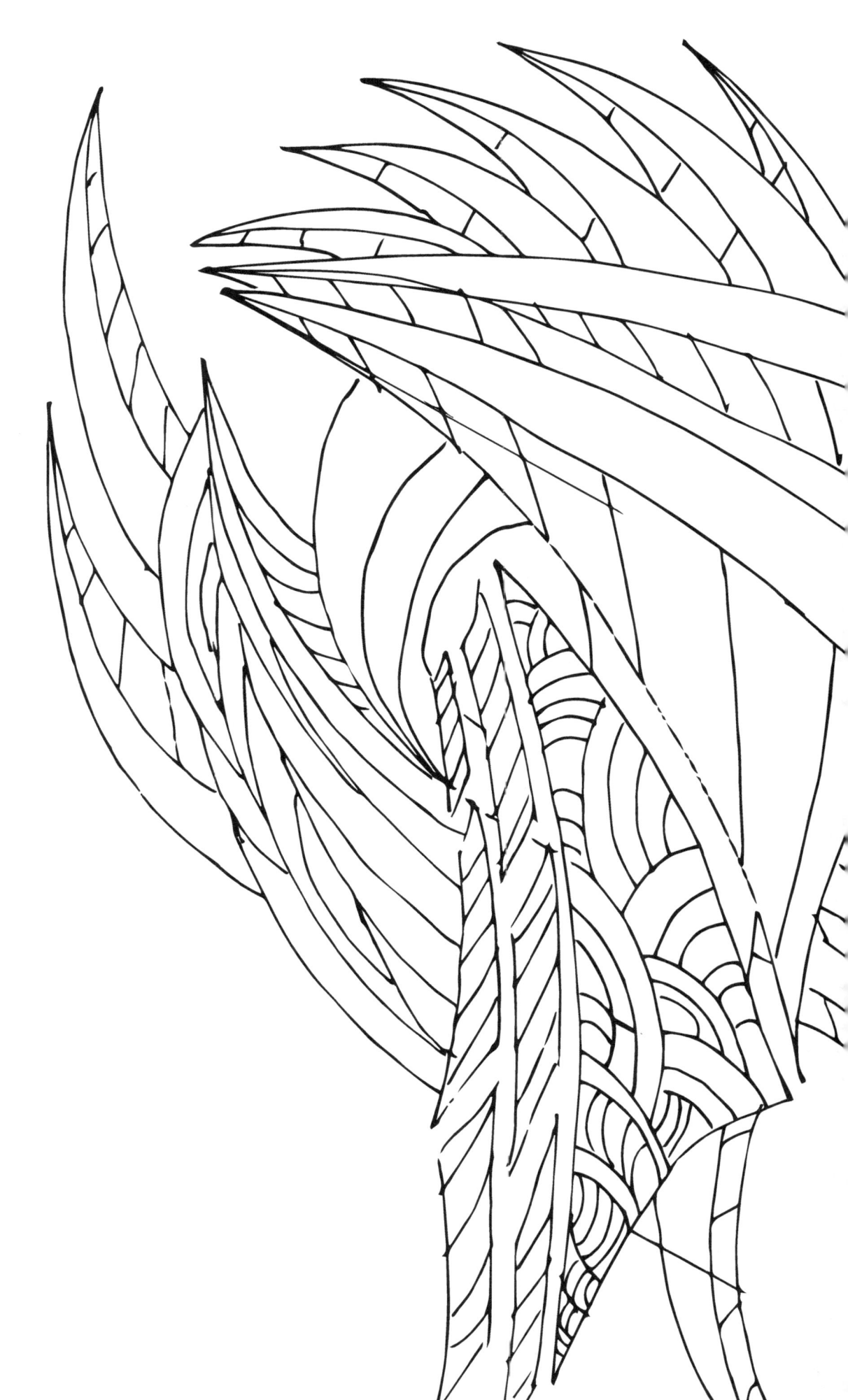

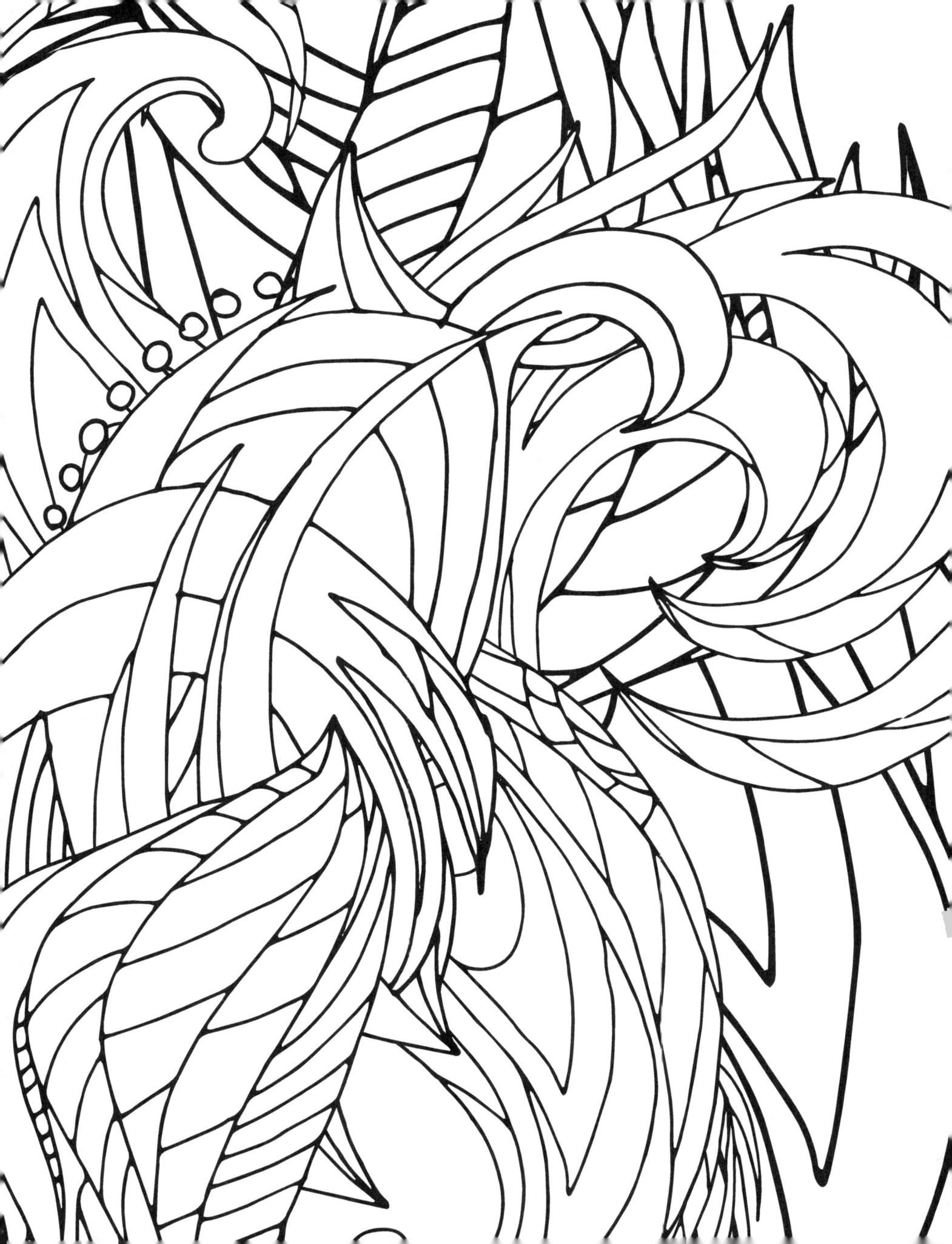

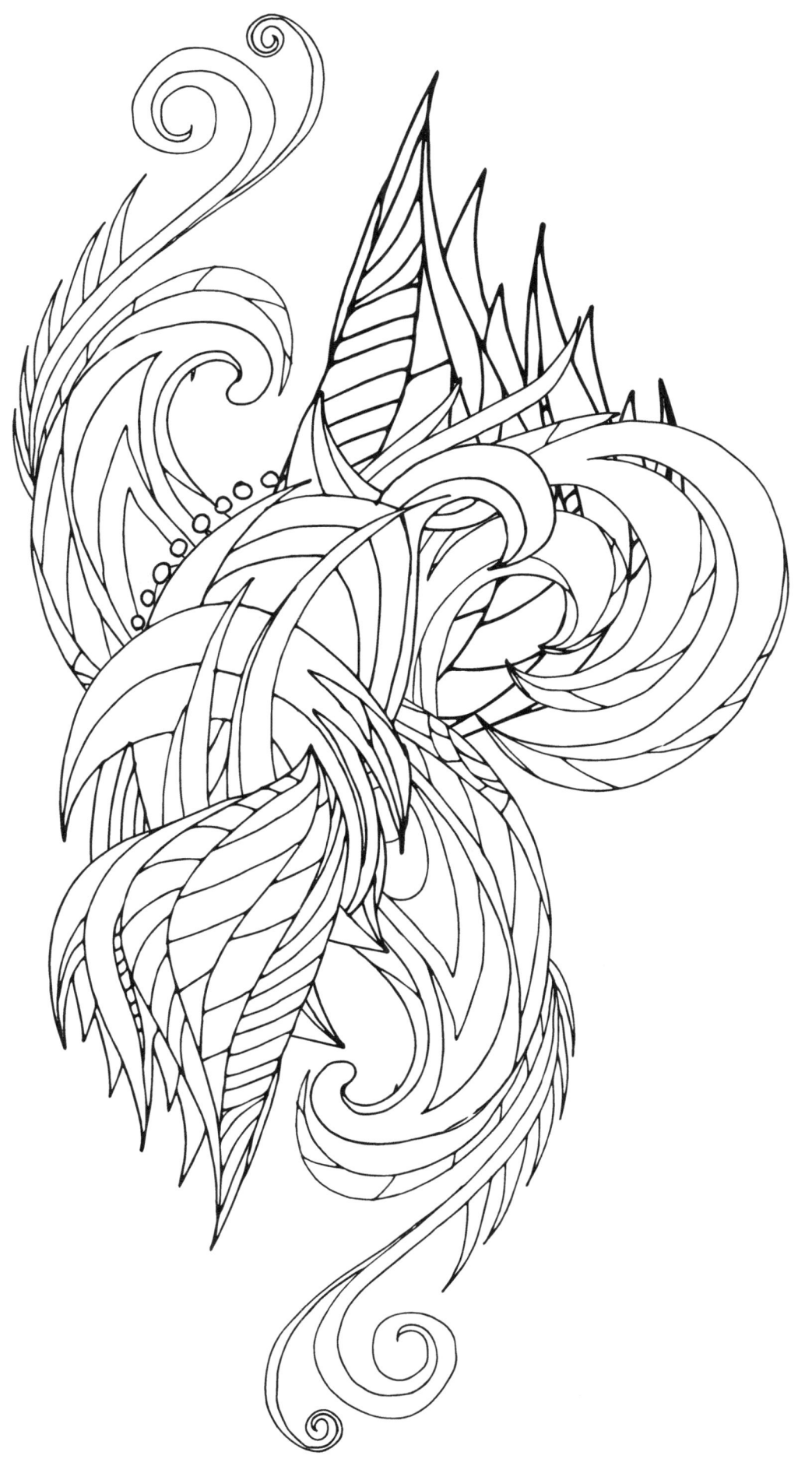

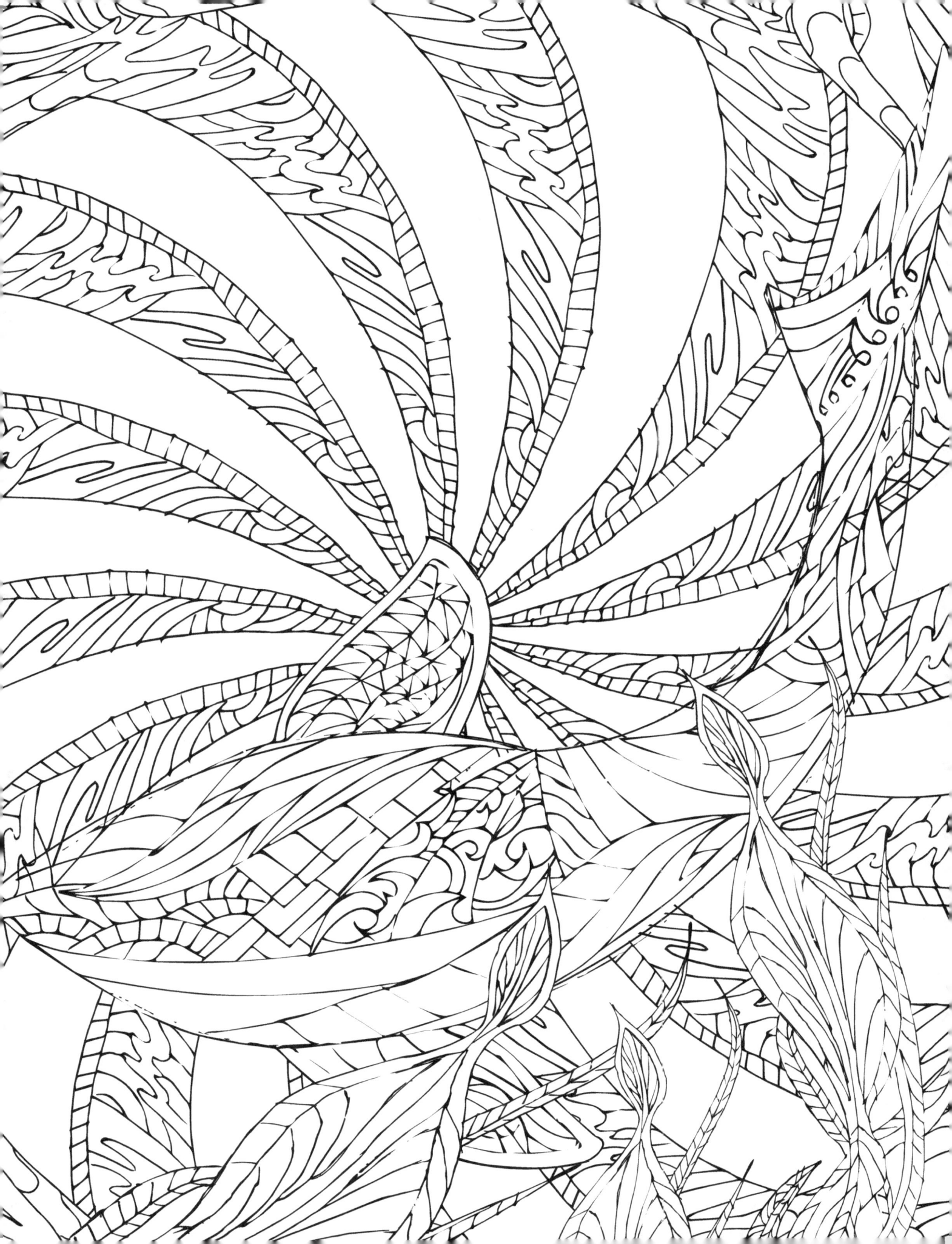

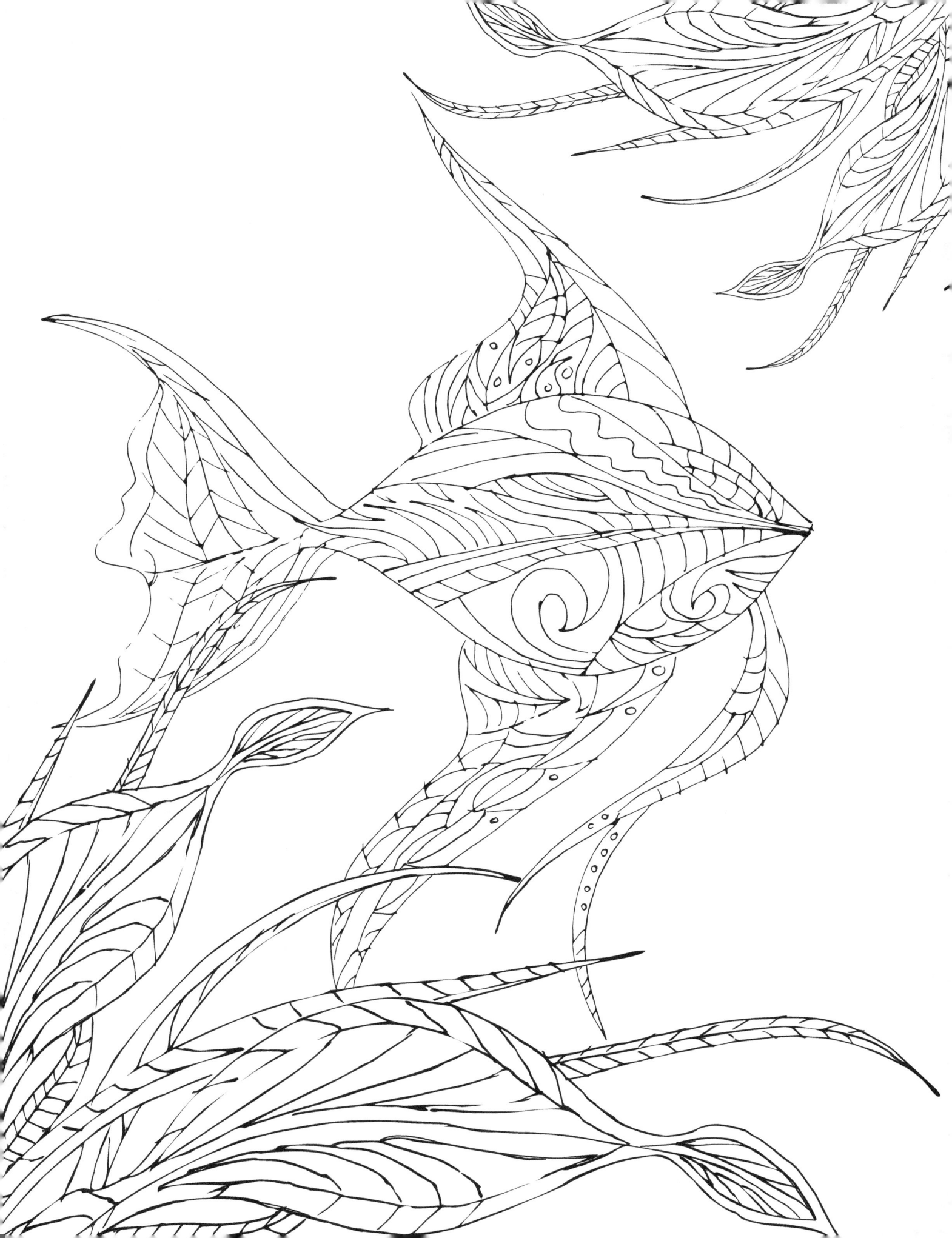

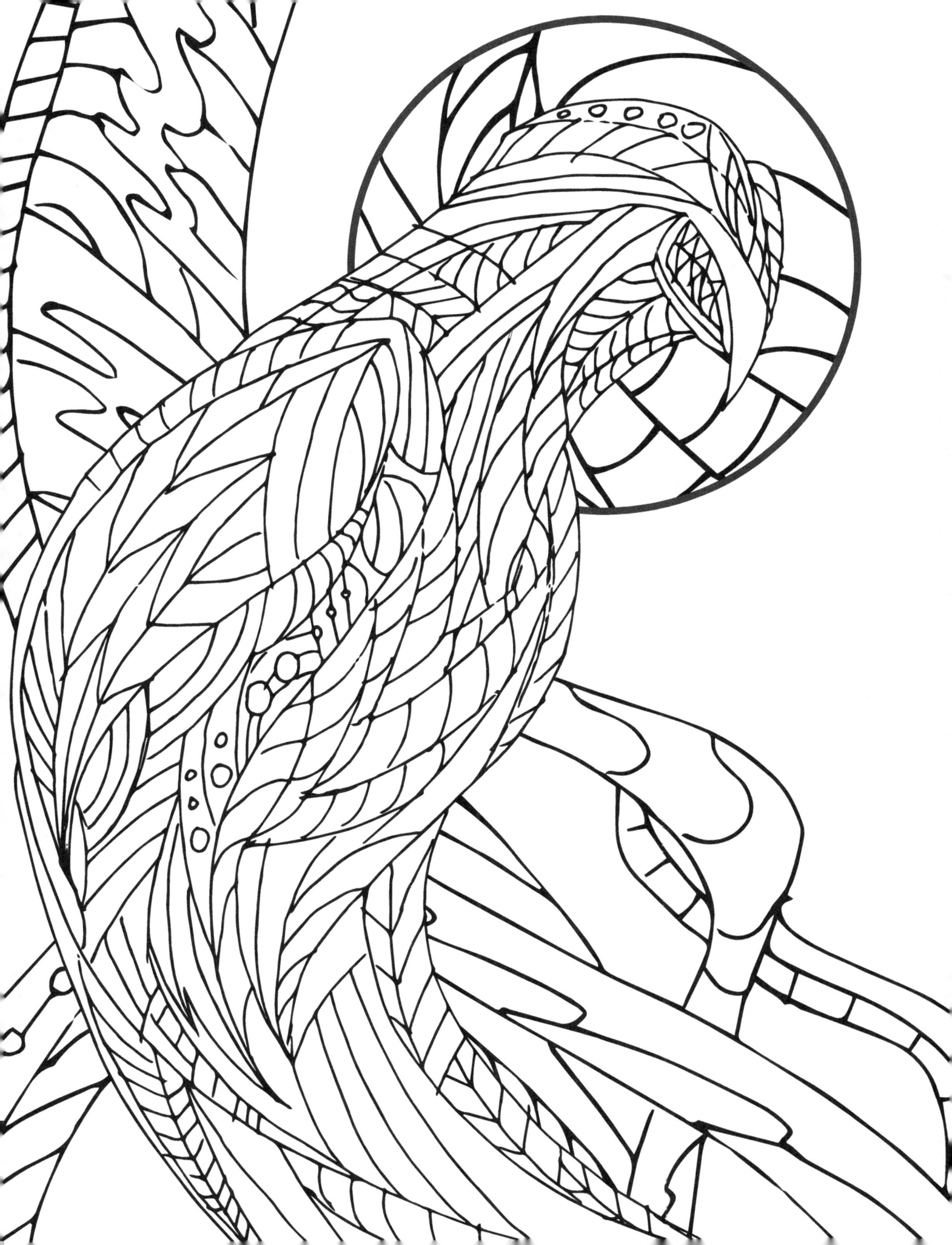

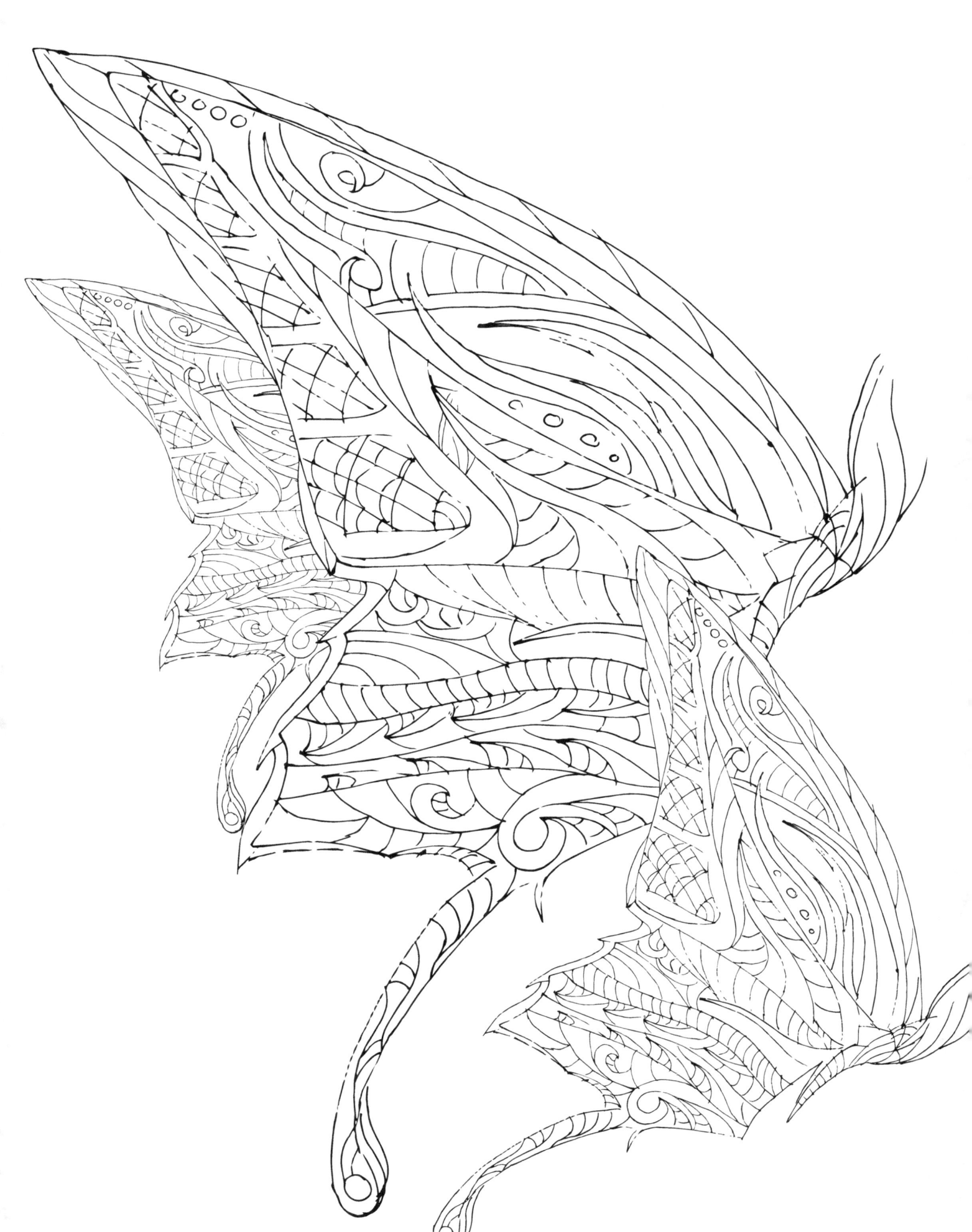

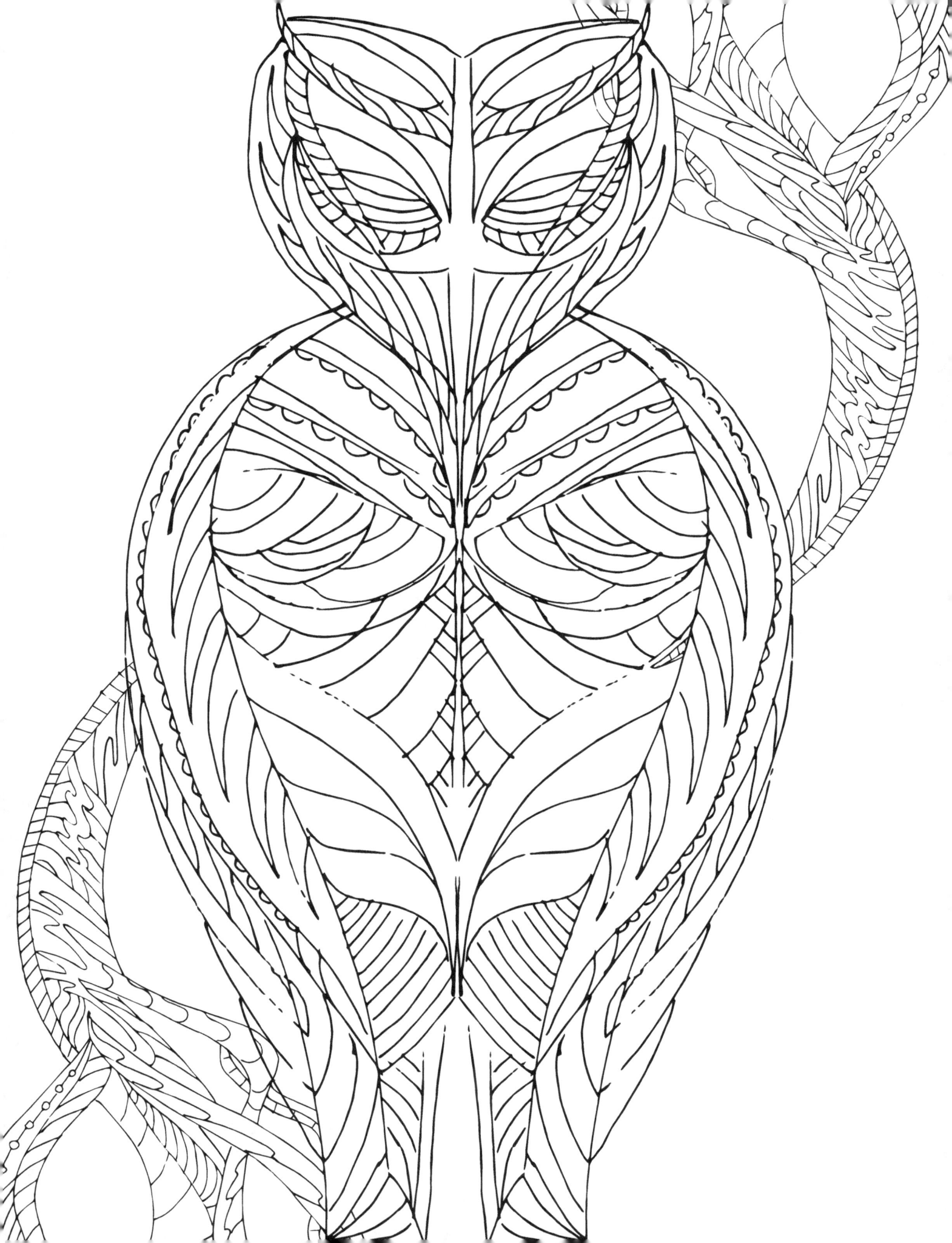

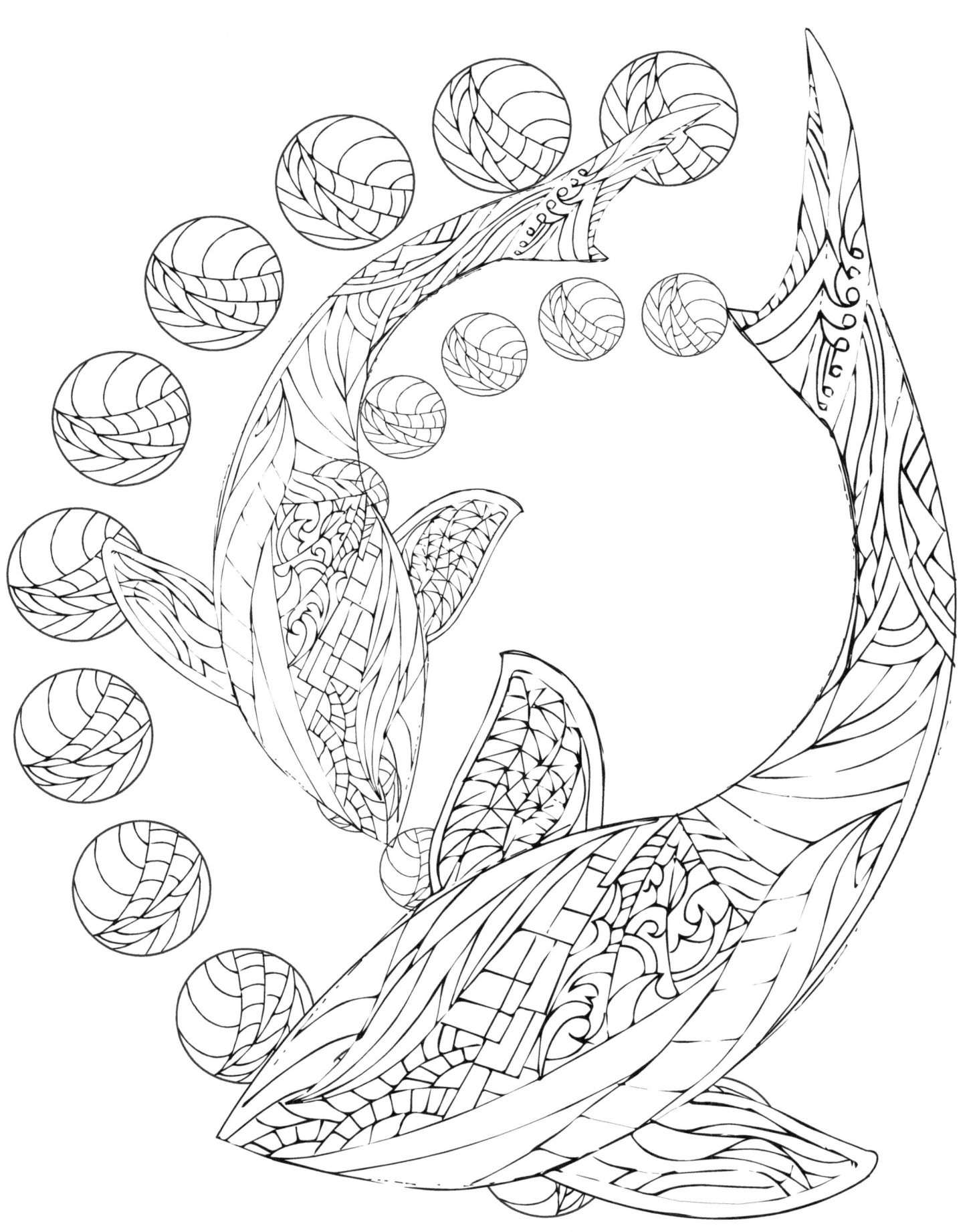

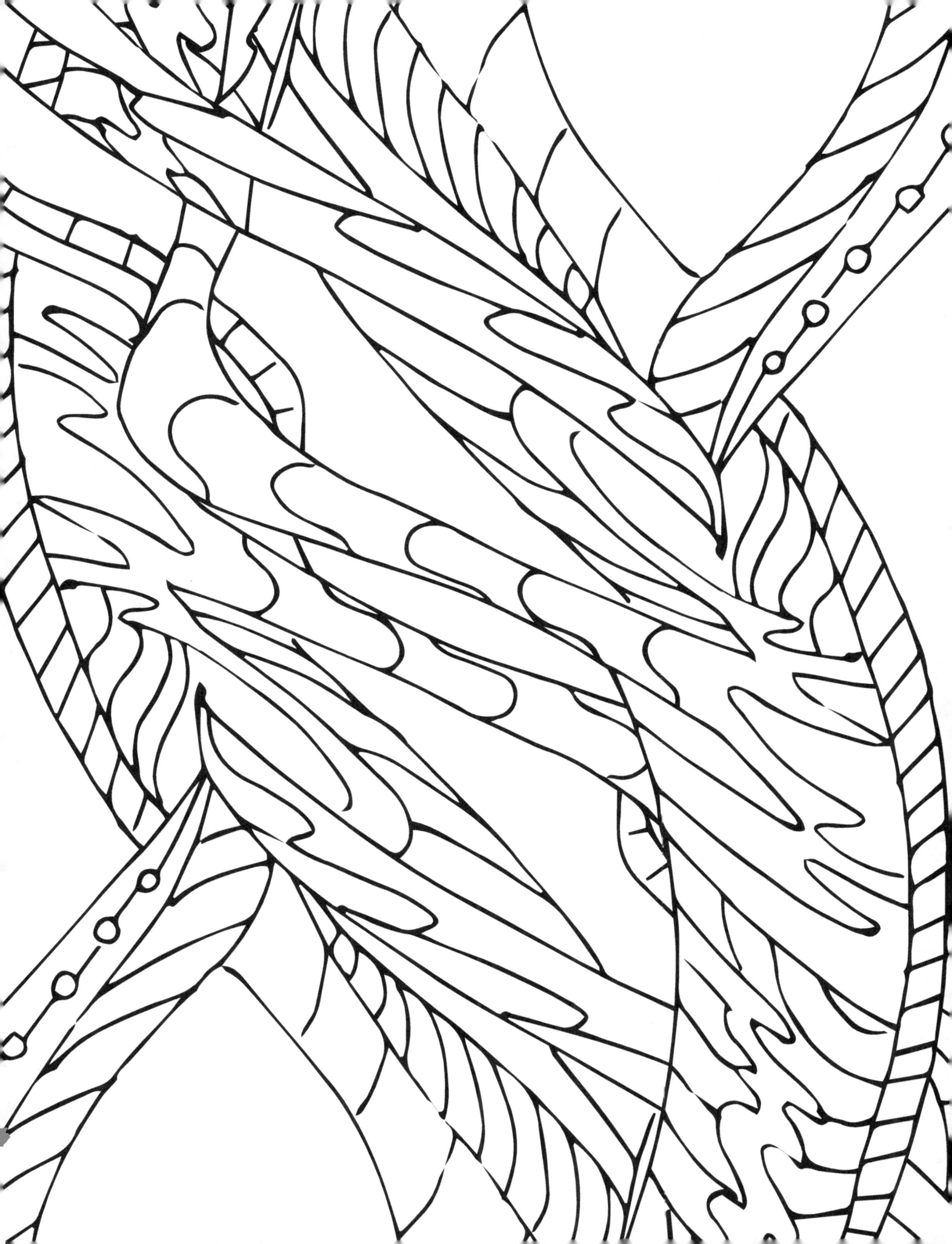

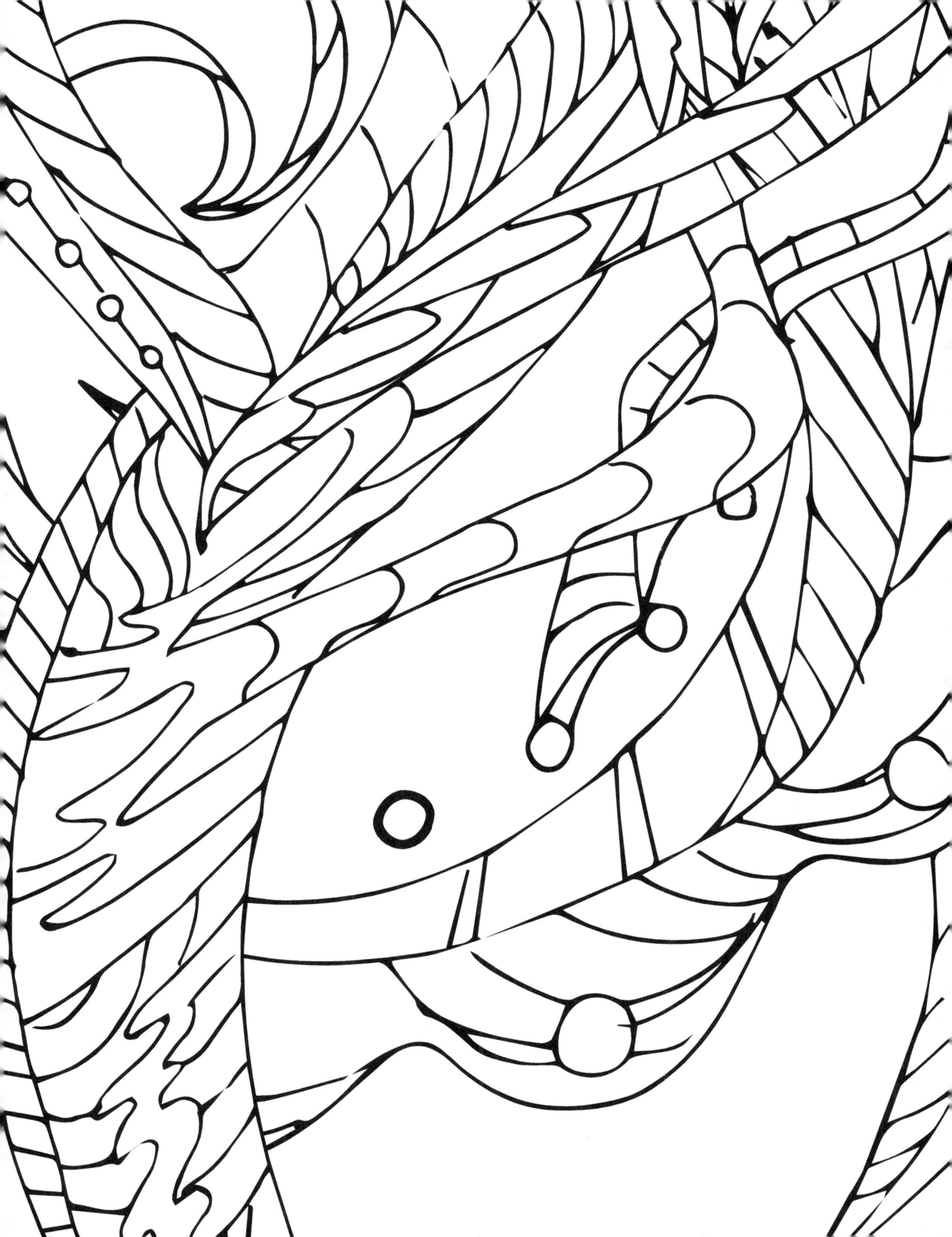

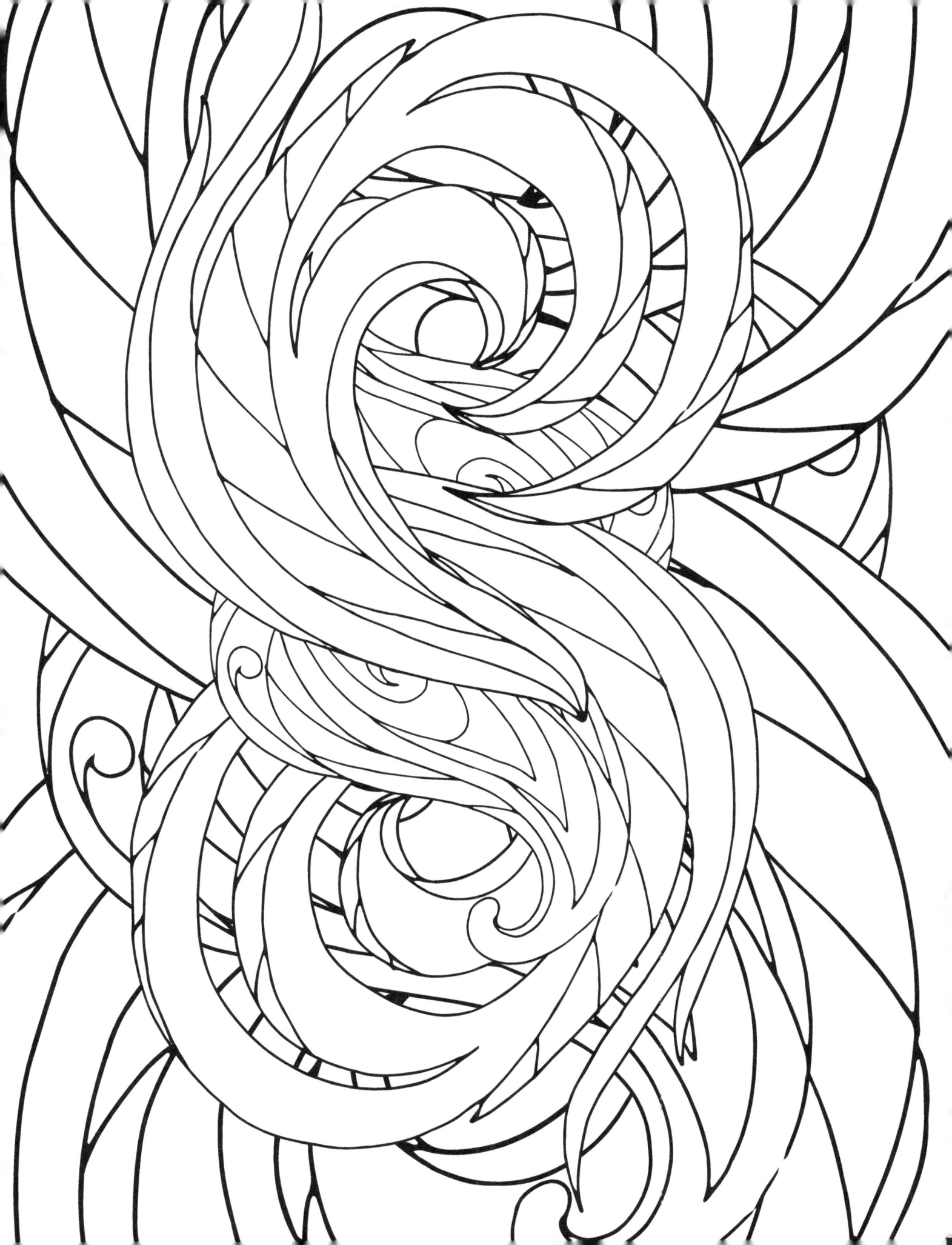

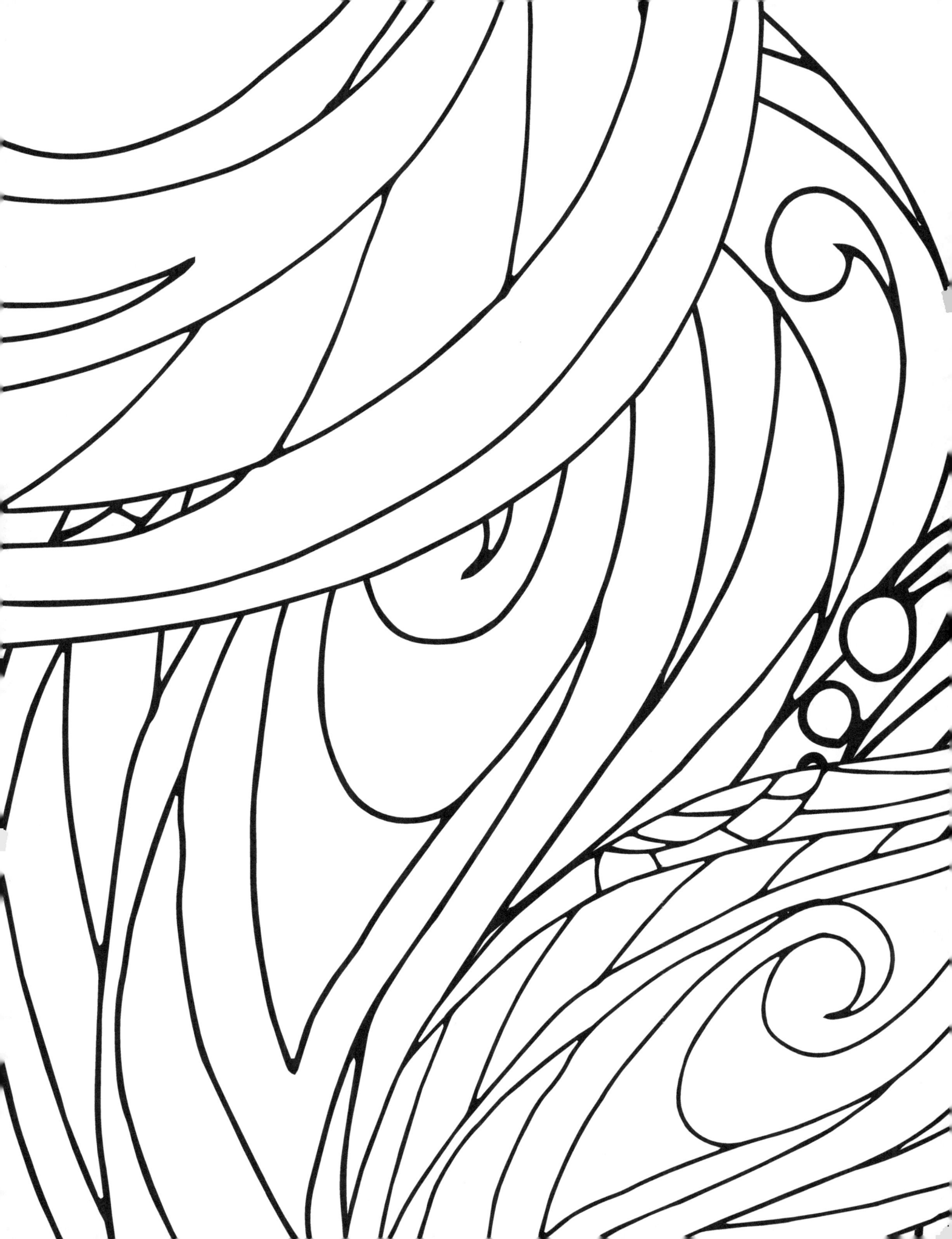

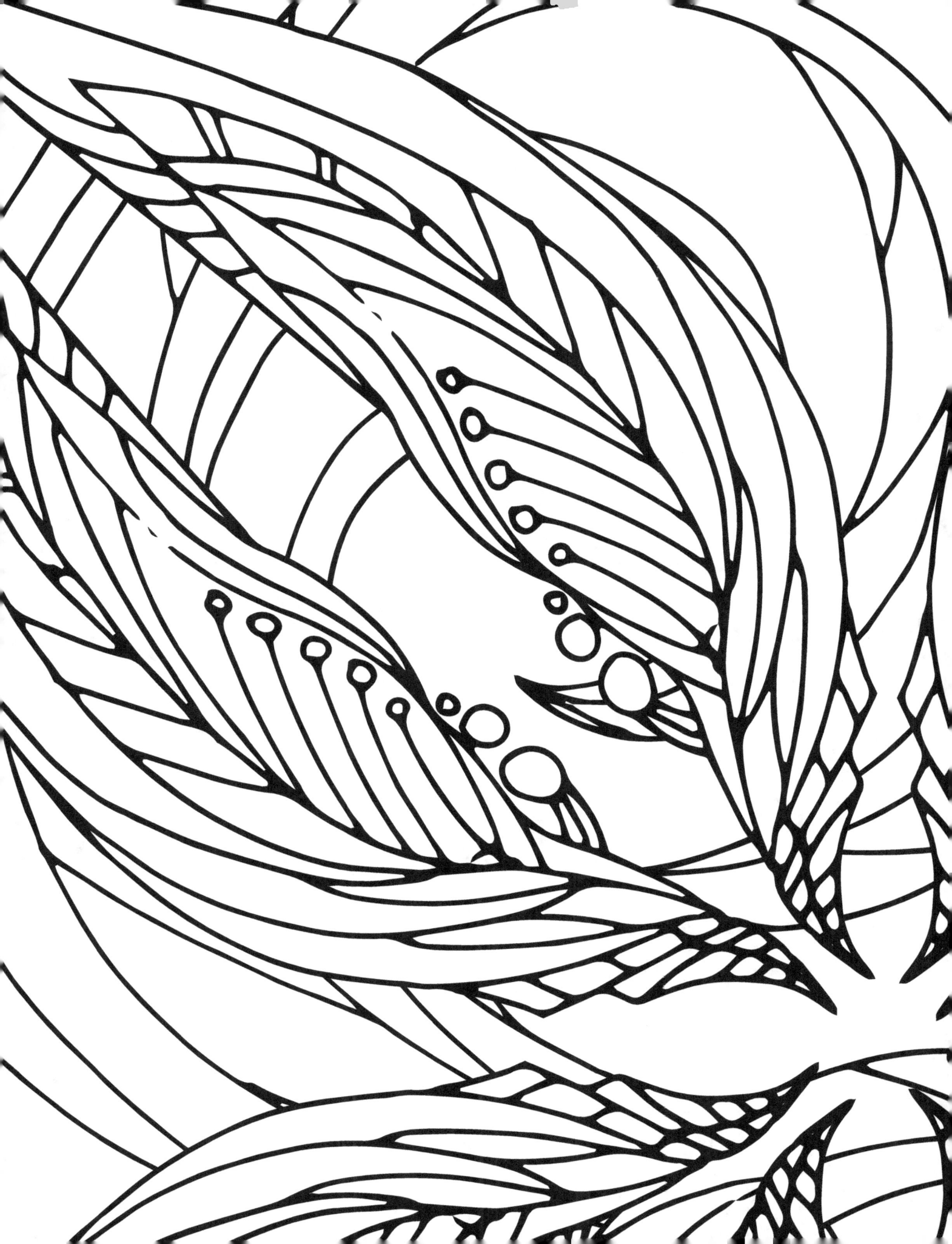

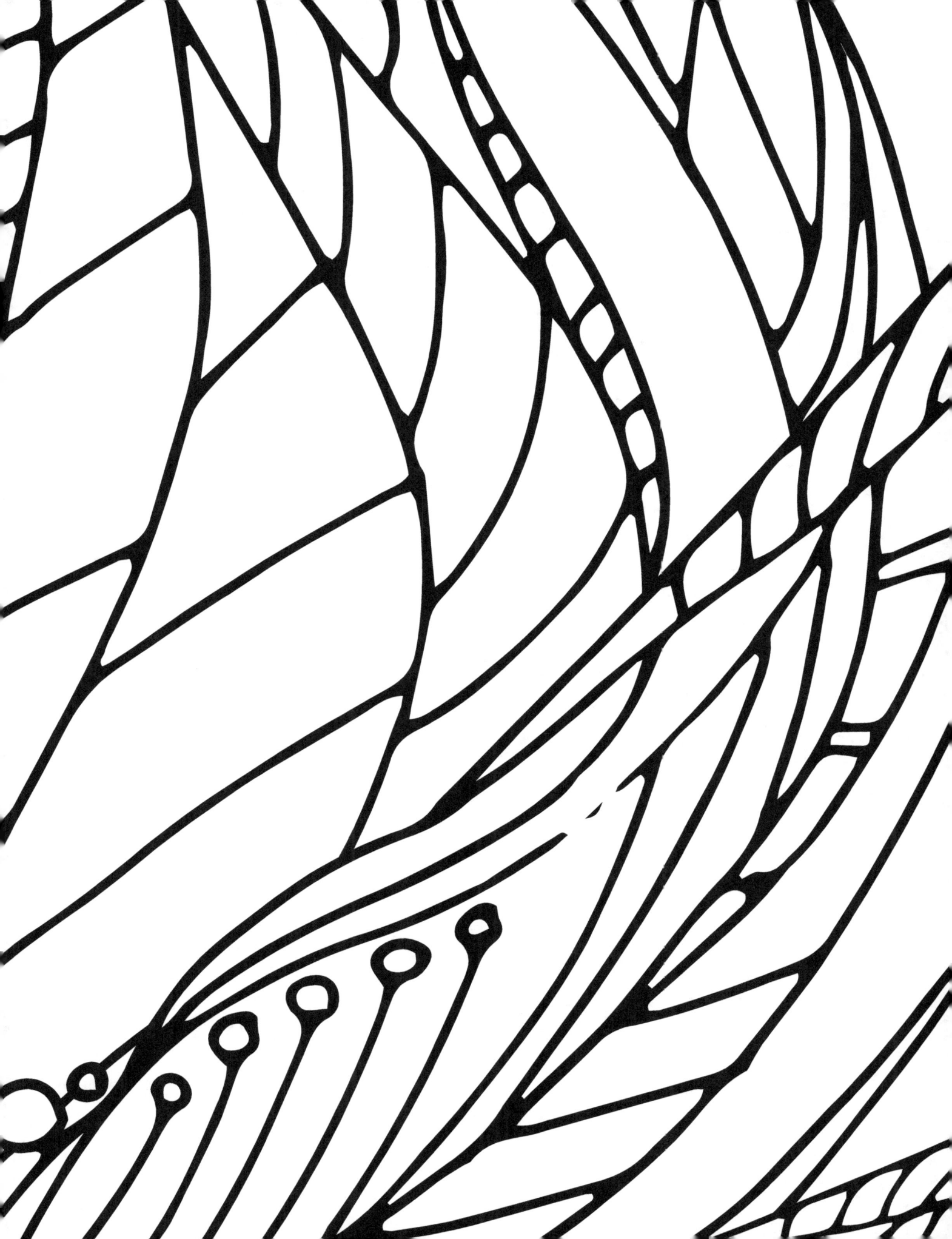

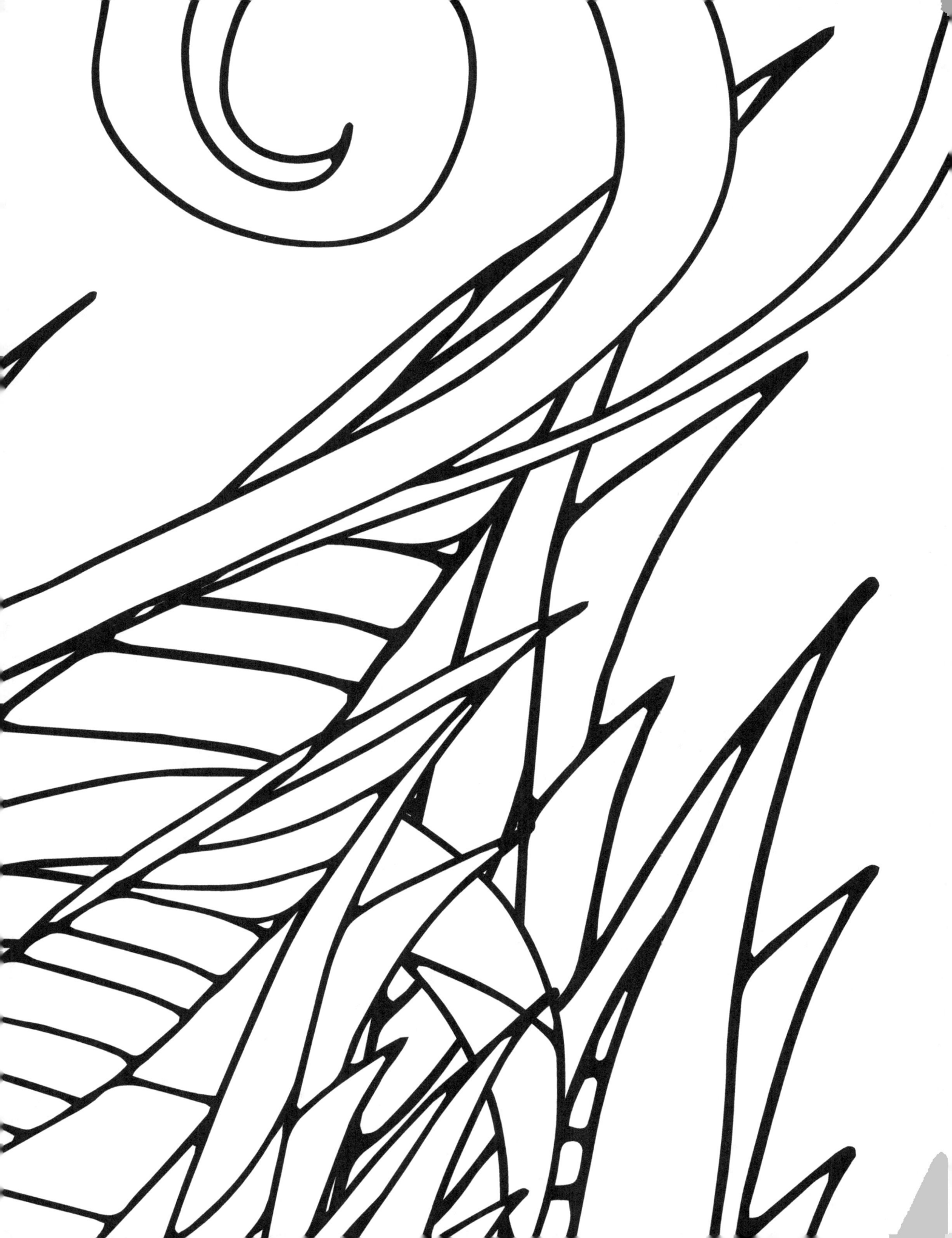

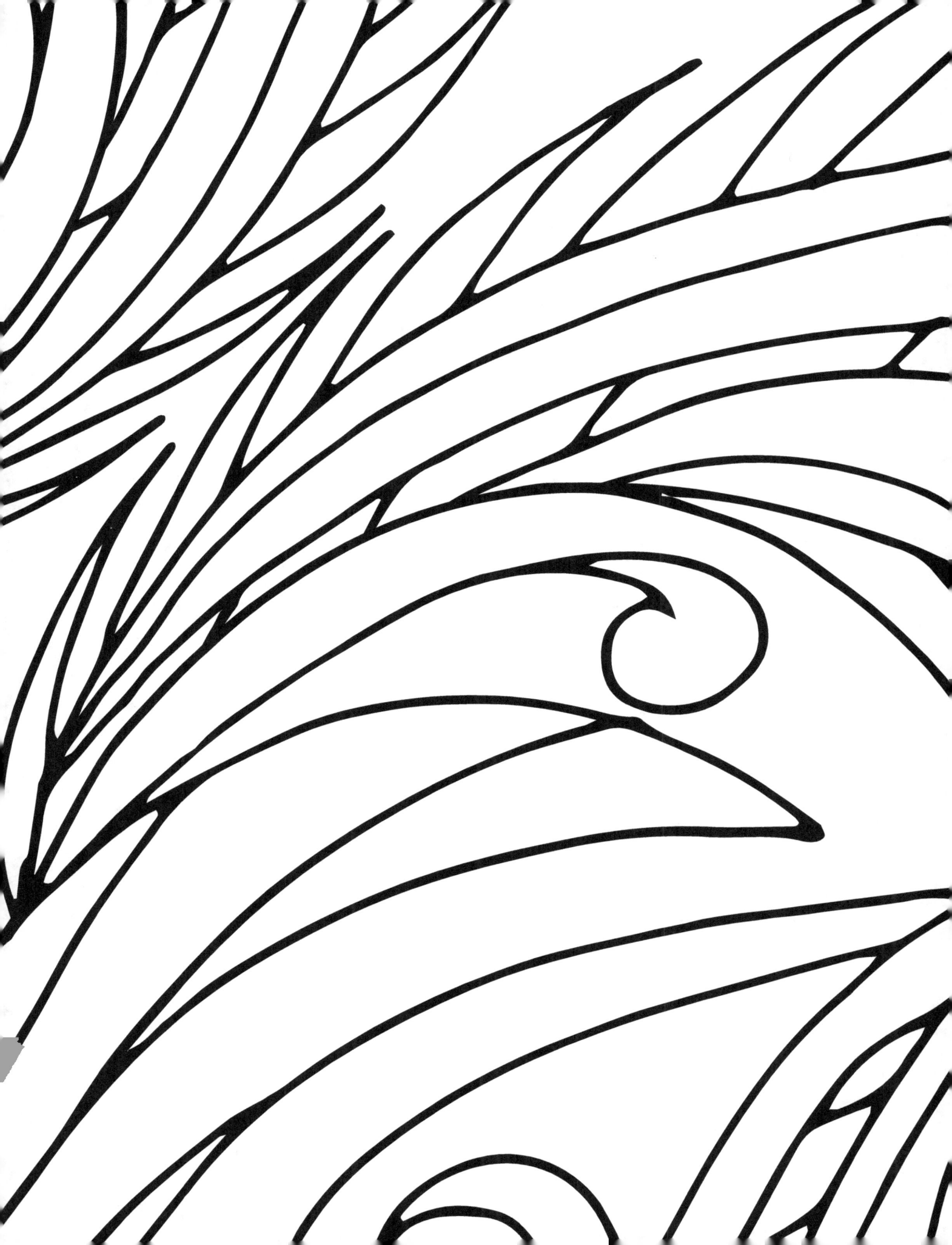

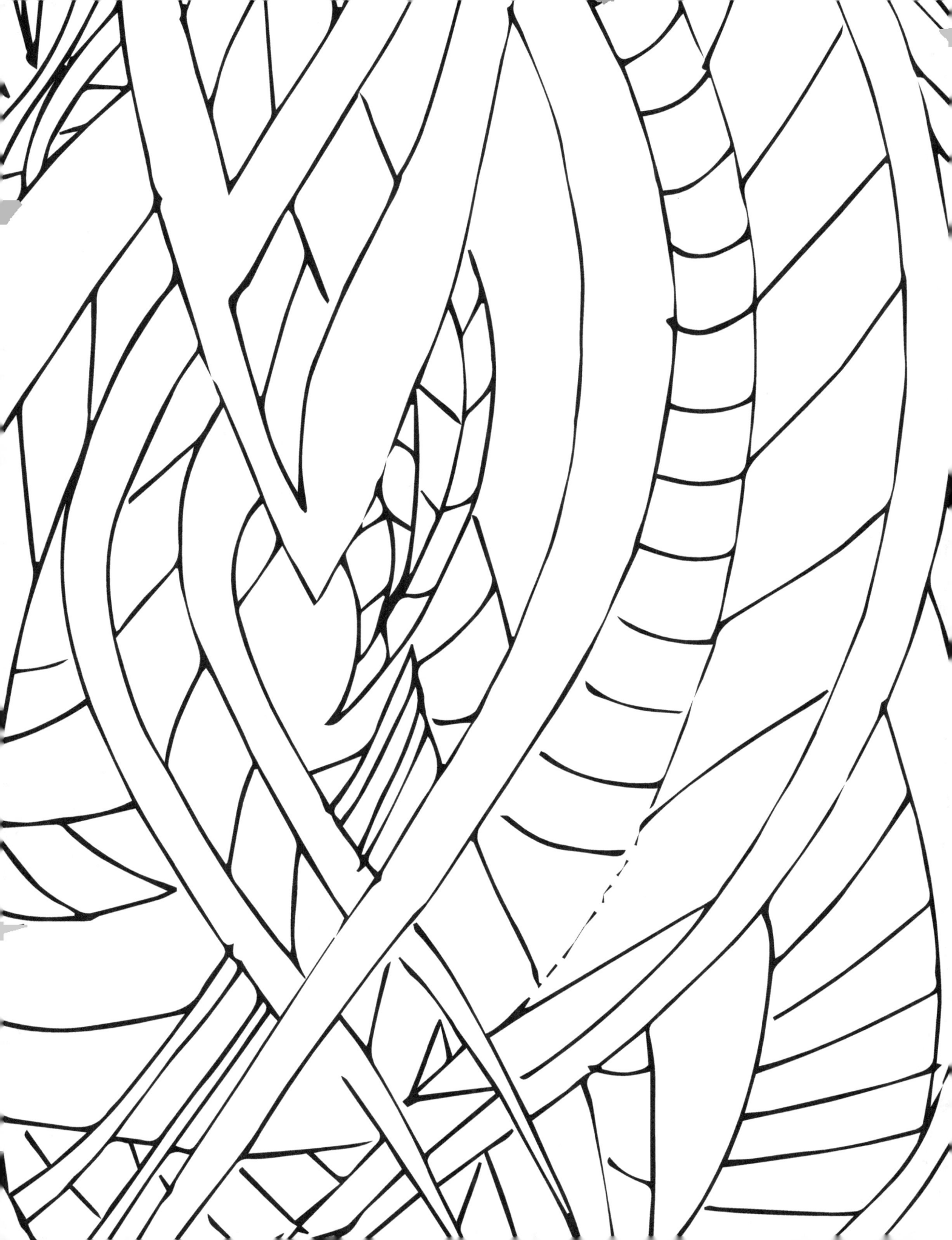

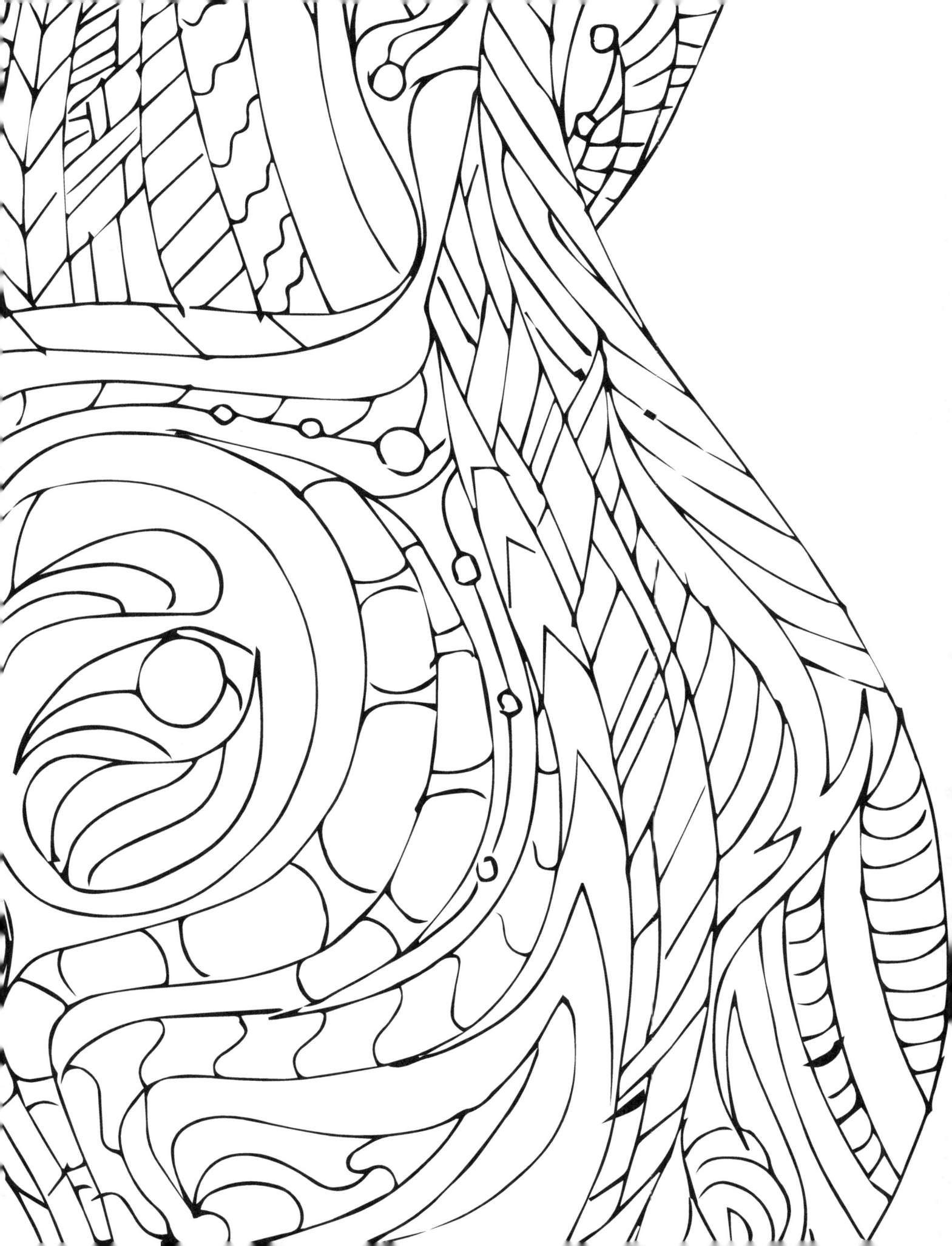

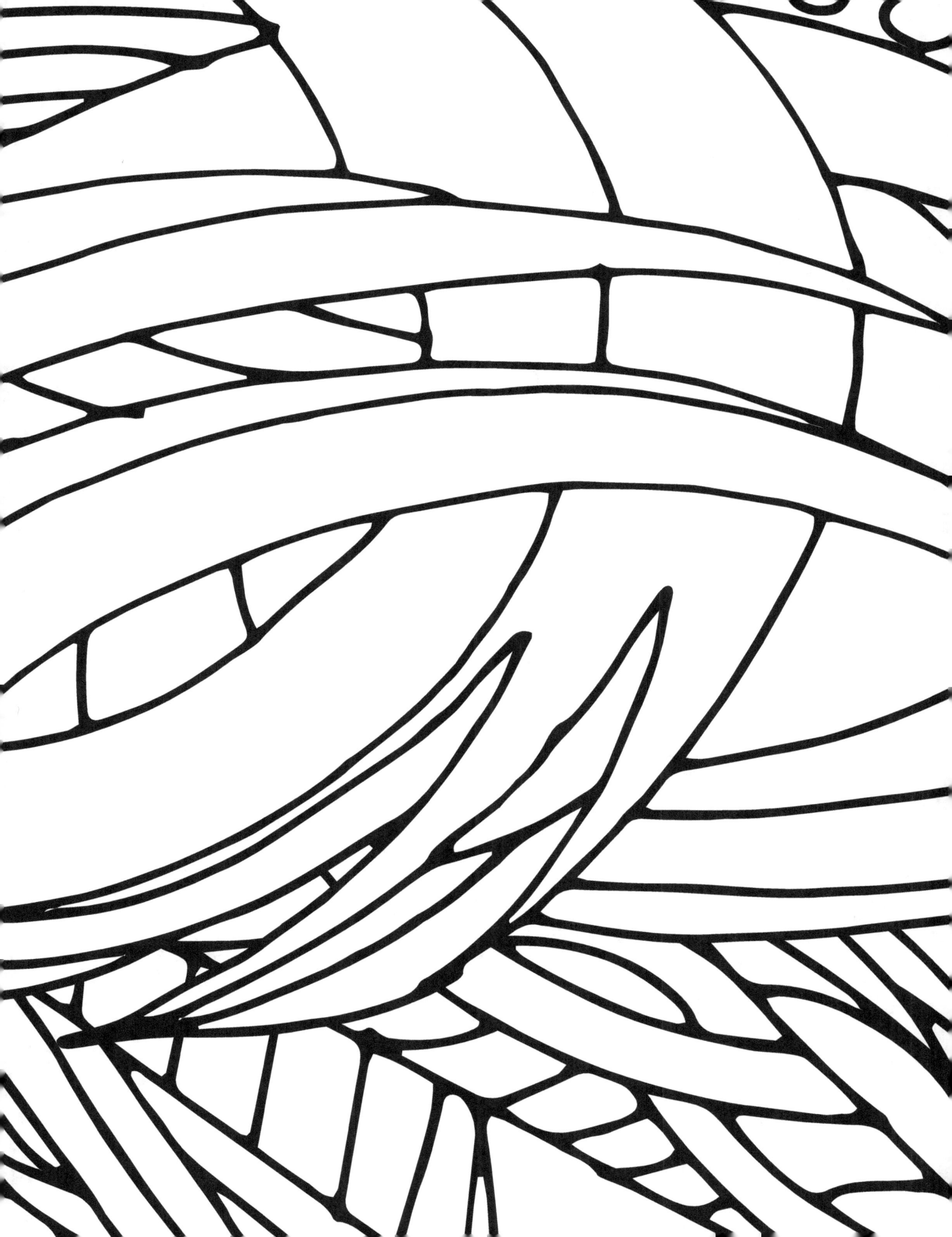

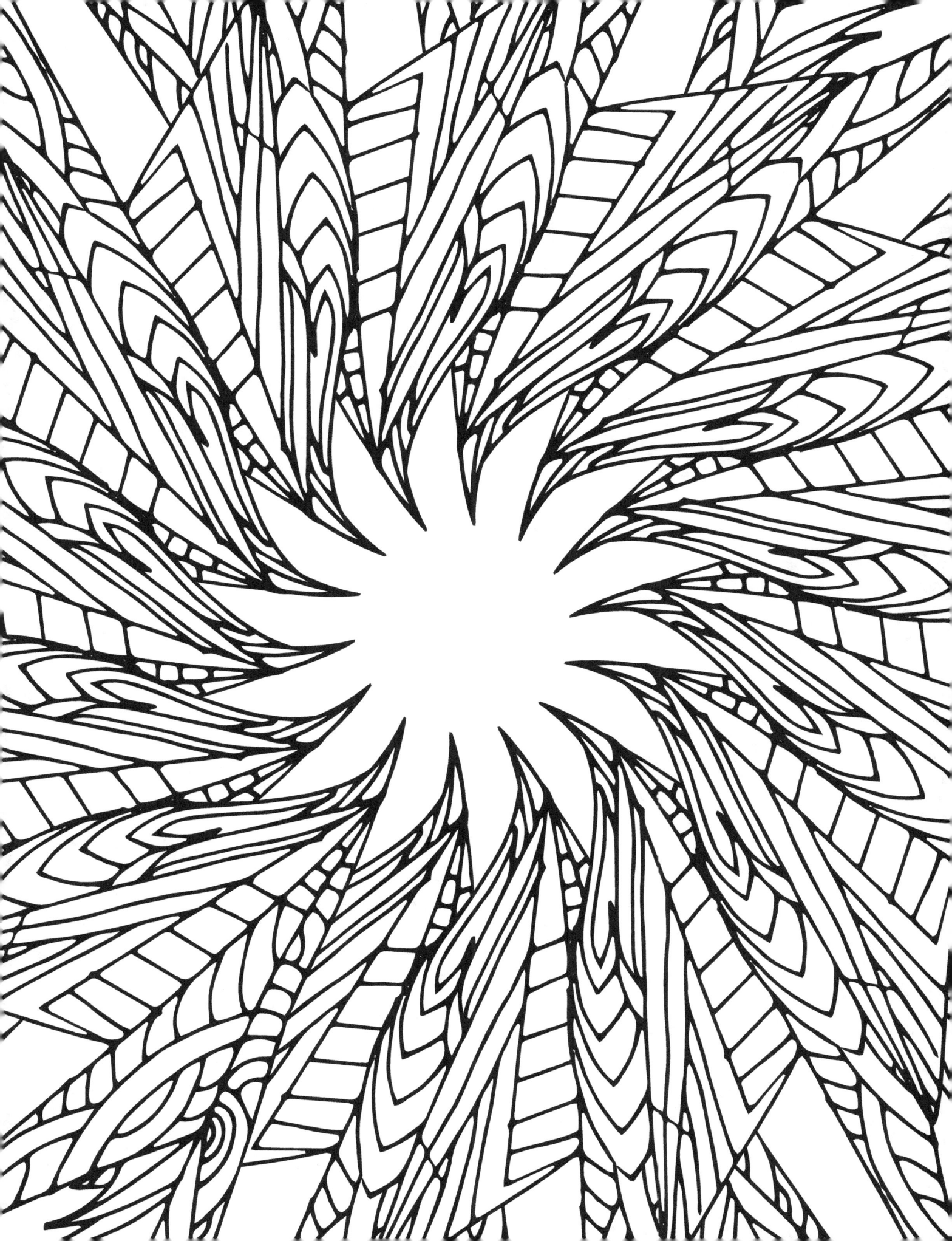

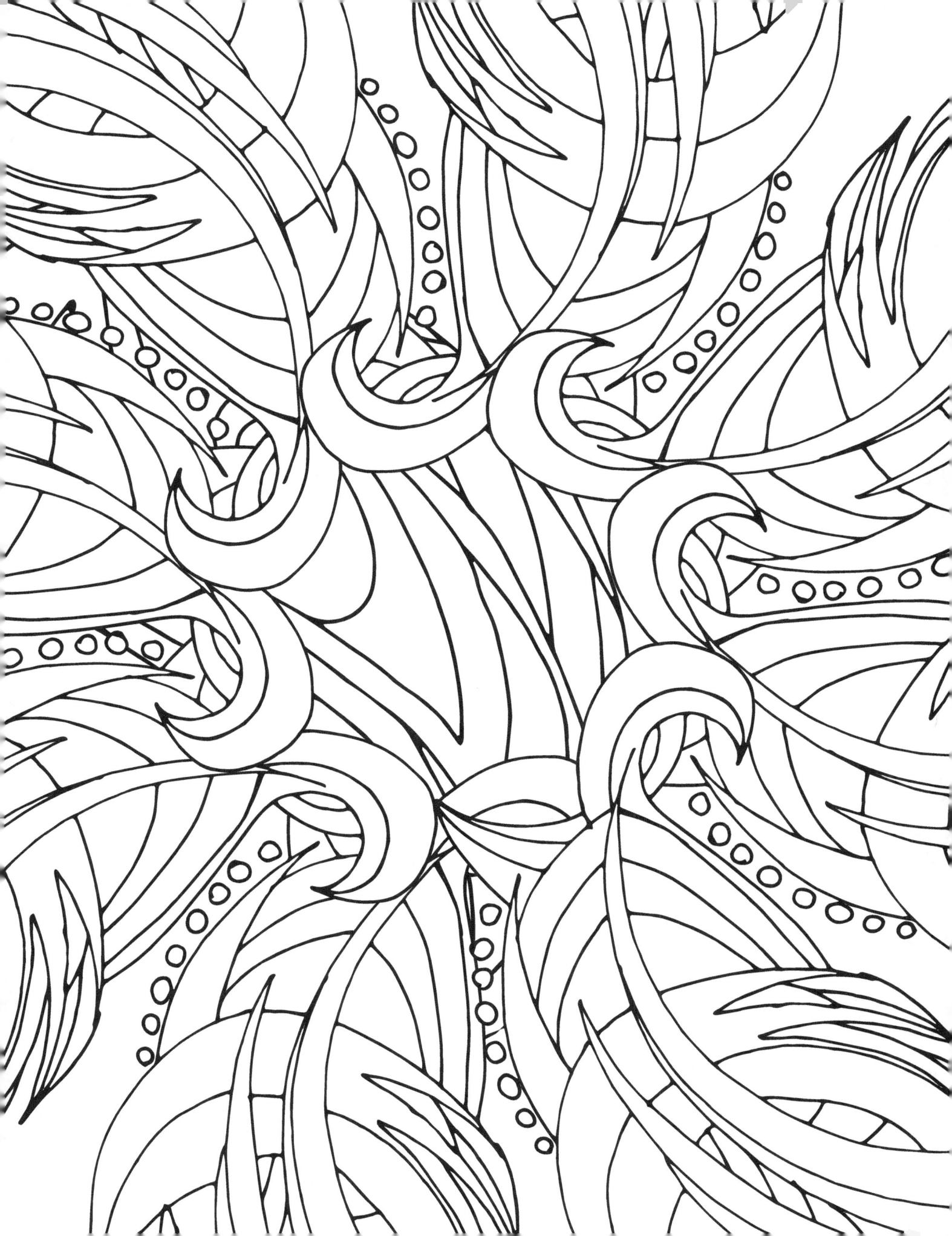

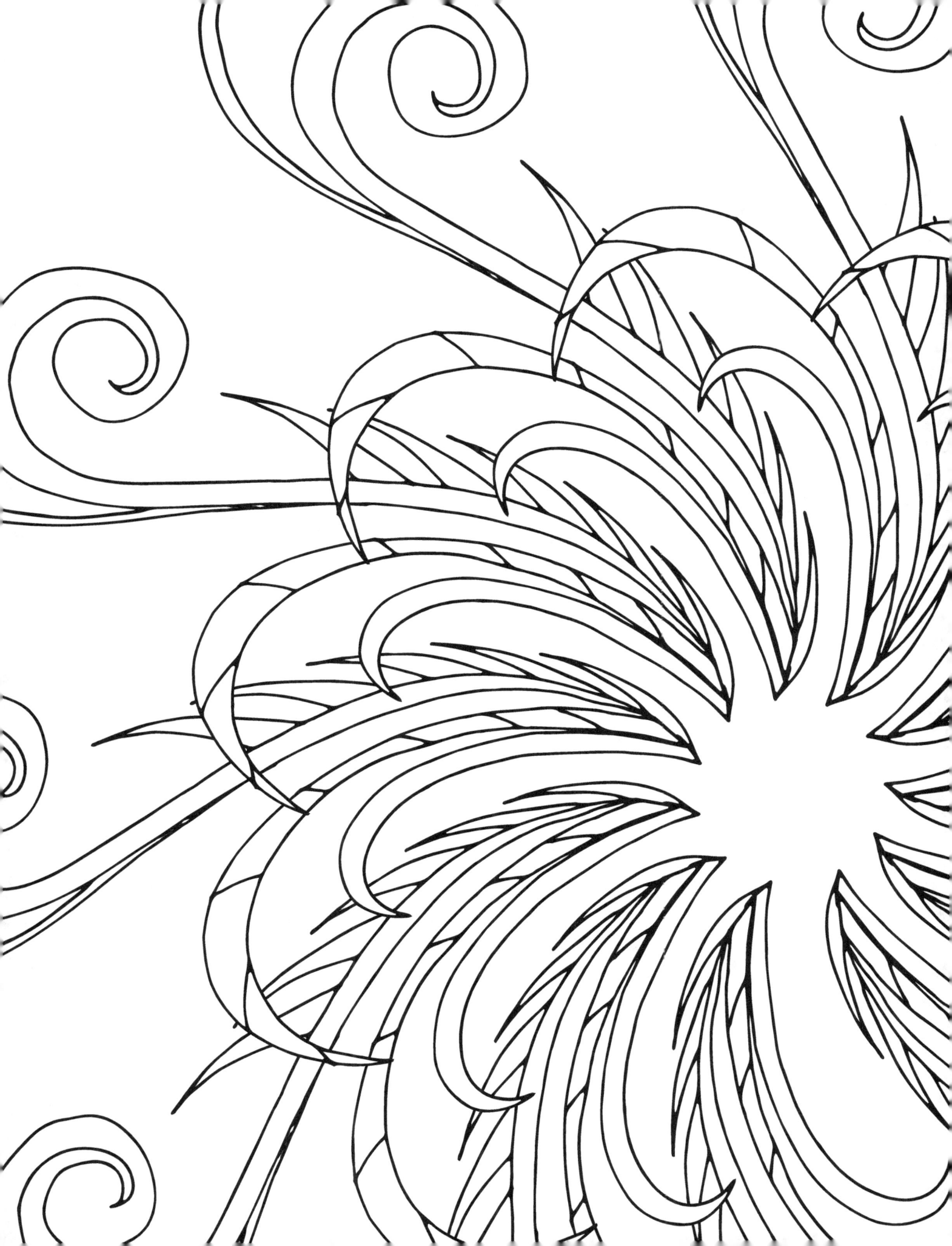

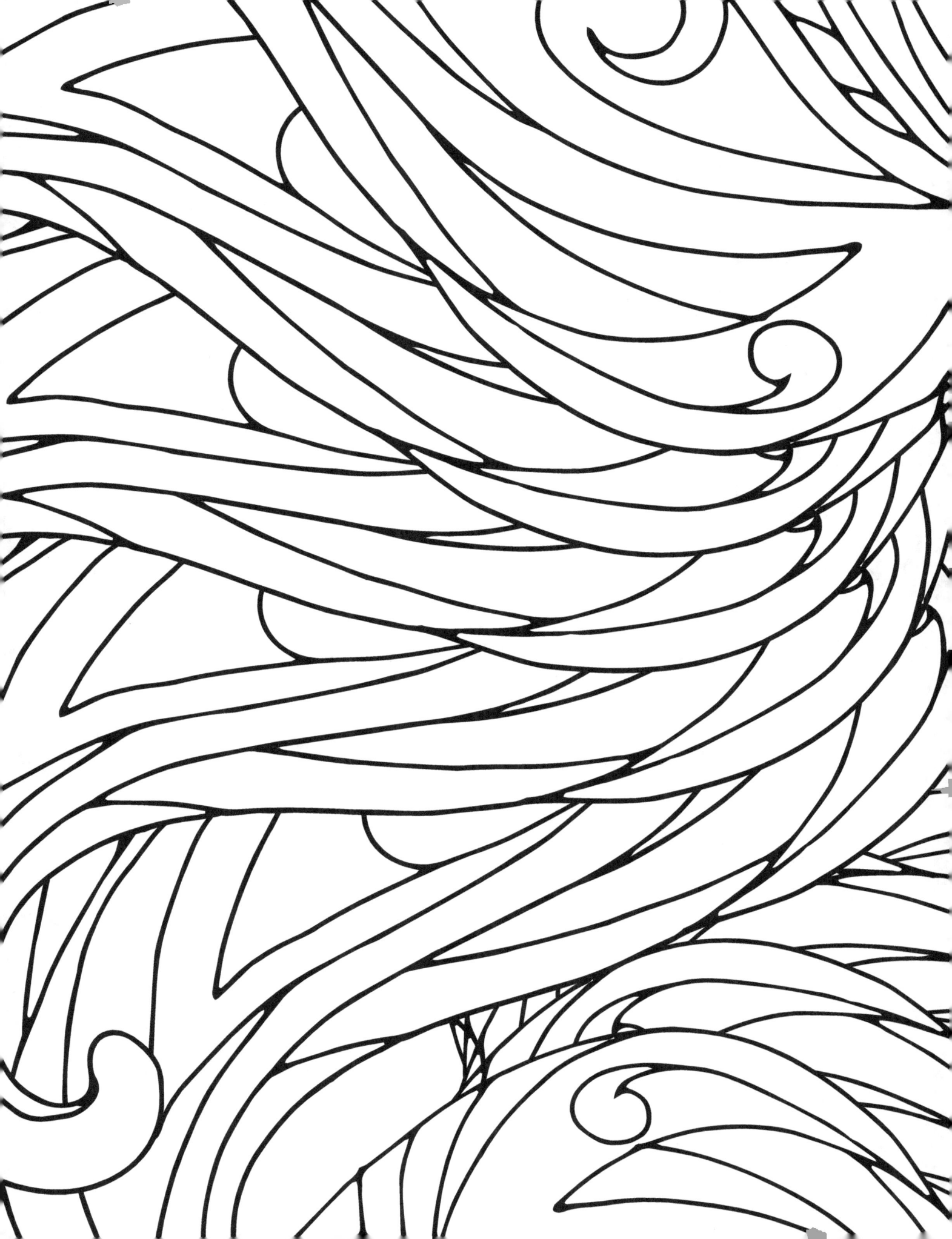

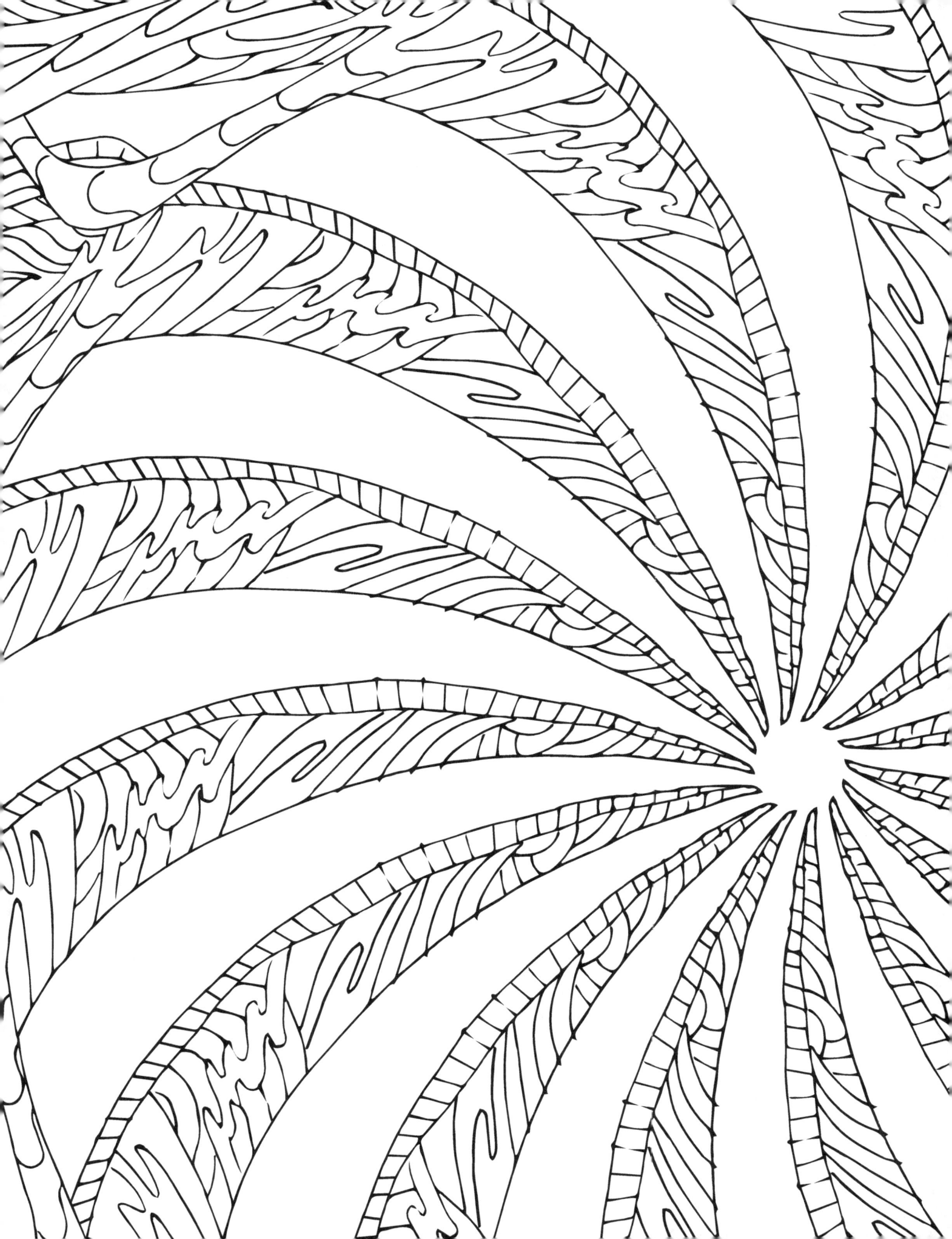

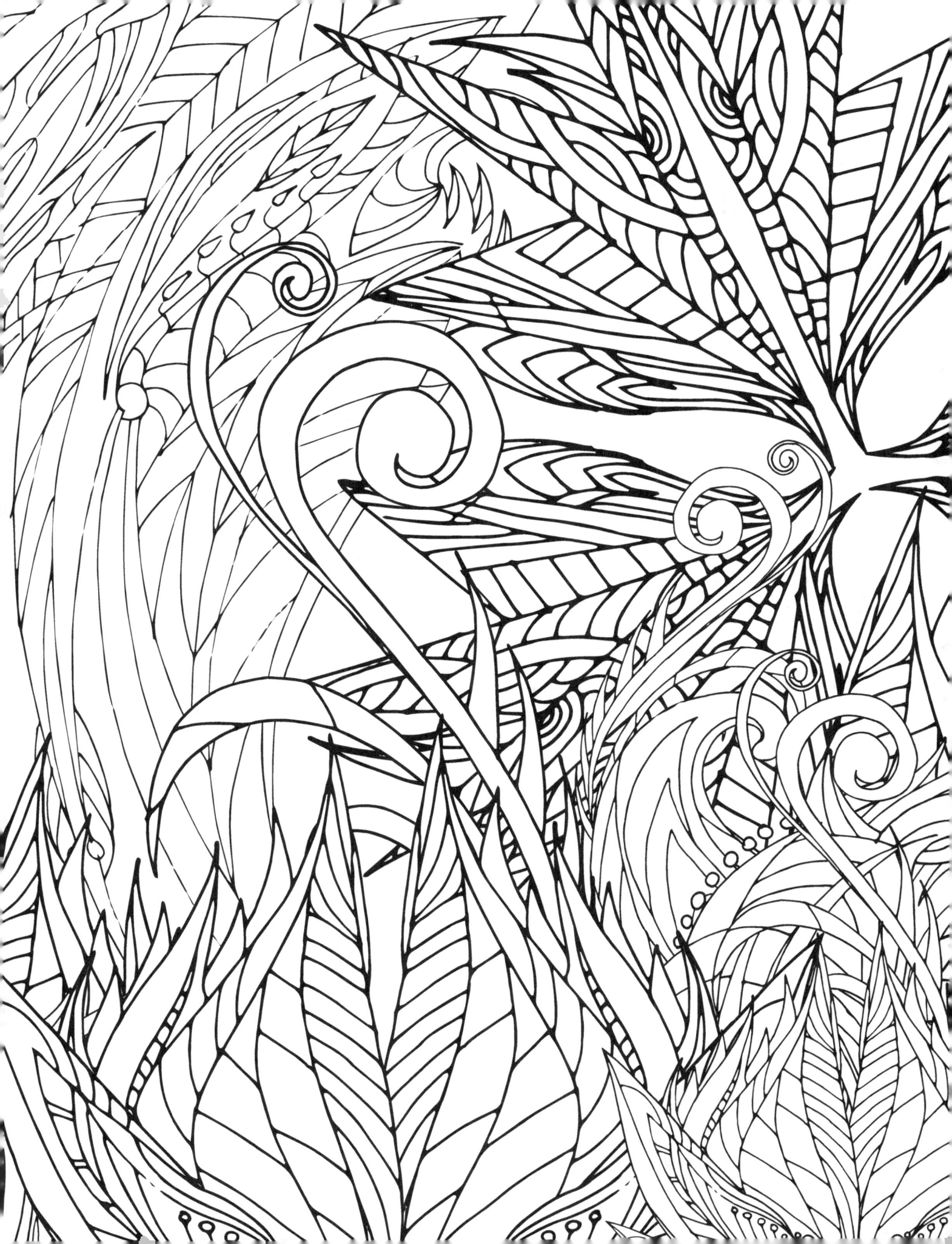

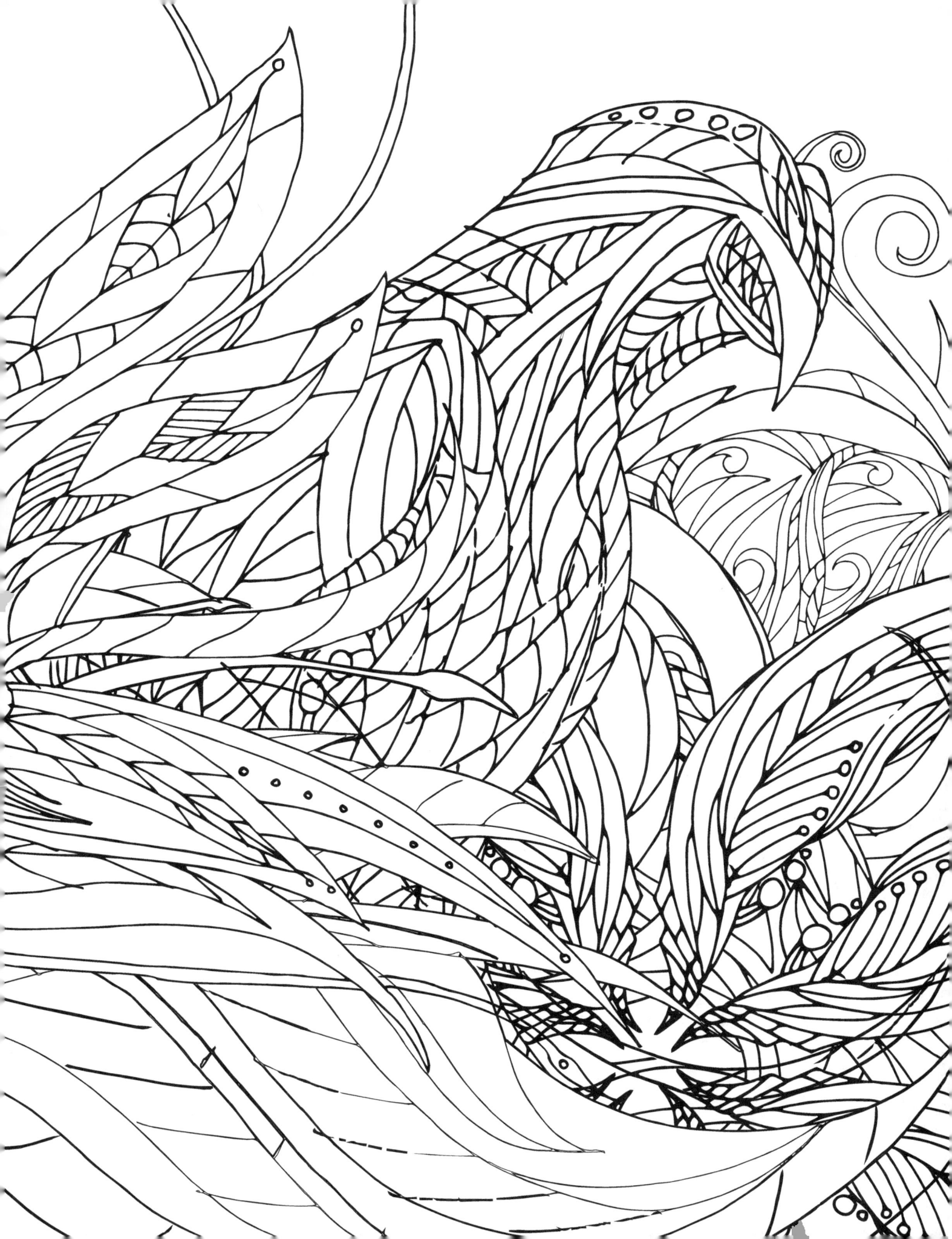

www.ingramcontent.com/pod-product-compliance
Lightning Source LLC
Chambersburg PA
CBHW08082118052 6
45168CB00006B/2536